THE
BULLDOG
AND THE
HELIX

THE BULLDOG

AND THE HELIX

DNA AND THE PURSUIT OF JUSTICE IN A FRONTIER TOWN

RAILWAY CROSSING

Shayne Morrow

VICTORIA
VANCOUVER
CALGARY

Heritage House Publishing Company Ltd.
heritagehouse.ca

Cataloguing information available from Library and Archives Canada

978-1-77203-250-5 (pbk)
978-1-77203-247-5 (epub)

Edited by Susan Safyan and Lenore Hietkamp
Proofread by Warren Layberry
Cover and interior design by Jacqui Thomas
Cover photographs: girl, by Alex Potemkin/iStockphoto.com;
street scene, courtesy of Alberni Valley Museum

The interior of this book was produced on 100% post-consumer recycled paper,
processed chlorine free, and printed with vegetable-based inks.

We acknowledge the financial support of the Government of Canada through
the Canada Book Fund (CBF) and the Canada Council for the Arts, and the
Province of British Columbia through the British Columbia Arts Council
and the Book Publishing Tax Credit.

23 22 21 20 19 1 2 3 4 5

Printed in Canada

Contents

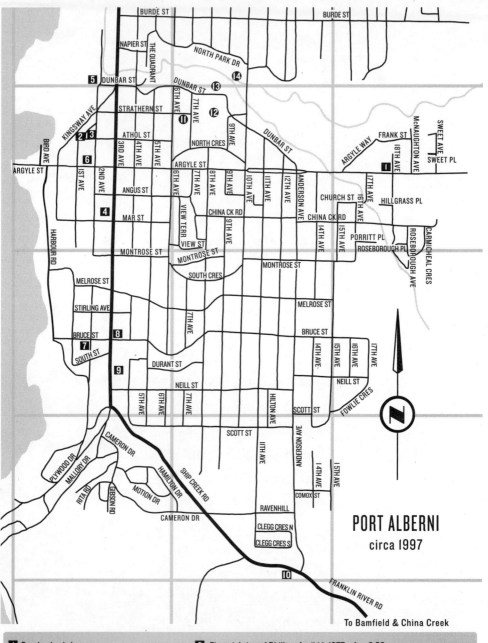

PORT ALBERNI

circa 1997

To Bamfield & China Creek

1 Carolyn Lee's house

2 Pat Cummings School of Dance

3 Arrowview Hotel

4 Pine Café

5 Alberni Foundry, owned by the Dhillons

6 Carolyn's usual walking route, where she was last seen on April 14, 1977, shortly after 6:30 PM

7 Gurmit Dhillon's house

8 First sighting of Dhillon, April 14, 1977, after 6:30 PM

9 Second sighting of Dhillon, April 14, 1977, after 6:30 PM

10 Route to potato field four kilometres down Franklin River Road, where Carolyn's body was found, April 15, 1977, around 5 PM

11 Jessica States's house

12 Athletic Park, where Jessica was last seen on July 31, 1996, around 9 PM

13 Spot where Patten meets Jessica

14 Dry Creek Park, where Jessica's body was found, August 1, 1996, 2:05 PM

Introduction

WHEN I MOVED to Port Alberni in early 1994, I had no idea that my adopted hometown had already become Canada's proving ground for forensic DNA law and technology. A brutal child sex slaying in April 1977 would become Canada's first historic DNA cold case, but first, Ottawa would have to write legislation to govern the use of this new genetic fingerprinting system. The technology to create DNA profiles from long-degraded samples was also still in development.

I was at my desk in the newsroom of the *Alberni Valley Times* in the fall of 1997 when I received a call from a documentary filmmaker for the Canadian Broadcasting Corporation (CBC), Jerry Thompson. The previous summer, an eleven-year-old girl named Jessica States had been savagely murdered just a few hundred metres from the *Times* office, in a wooded gully across the street from Recreation Park. On the night of the crime, there was a well-attended men's fast-pitch tournament at the park, and Jessica, who lived nearby, was on hand, retrieving foul-ball shots that flew into the gully.

When conventional investigation techniques failed to turn up the suspect, the Royal Canadian Mounted Police (RCMP) launched a DNA manhunt, eventually taking blood samples, mostly voluntary, from hundreds of men who were known to be at the park that night. Thompson had received a tip that the case was about to break, and he wanted to make a one-hour segment for the CBC Television series *Witness*.

On July 31, 1996, the night Jessica was killed, I was a forty-three-year-old rookie reporter, and the *Alberni Valley Times* had three industry veterans who handled the bulk of the early coverage. But by the time the States investigation shifted into a DNA manhunt, I had emerged as the primary court and crime reporter. It may be pure coincidence, but I was born on February 28, 1953, the day James Watson and Francis Crick published their findings on the DNA molecule—the double helix that gives this book its name. When I first encountered DNA science while in high school in the late 1960s, I was hooked.

In December 1996, the Port Alberni detachment commander, Inspector Andy Murray, arranged a private tour for me at the RCMP's E Division forensic lab in Vancouver, where I brushed up on the latest forensic DNA methodology with specialist Stefano Mazzega. At the time, the RCMP was just making the transition from the original DNA "fingerprinting" system known as Restriction Fragment Length Polymorphism (RFLP) to Polymerase Chain Reaction (PCR), which allows investigators to process much smaller amounts of trace material by making duplicates of the targeted genes.

When Thompson contacted me in 1997, I had to tell him that the States investigation had gone cold again. But Port Alberni RCMP had another DNA case in progress. The previous March, they had announced the arrest of forty-seven-year-old Gurmit Singh Dhillon for the slaying of Carolyn Lee in 1977. When investigators submitted genetic samples taken from the crime scene to the new PCR analysis, the Mounties finally had their man.

Why not, I suggested to Thompson, work backward through the Carolyn Lee murder case, while at the same time working forward on the Jessica States case? And if nothing breaks on the States investigation, load everything into the Lee case.

And that is how things played out. As the States investigation dragged on and the Dhillon case proceeded to trial, Thompson crafted a one-hour segment titled "The Gene Squad," which told the Port Alberni story in tandem with a successful DNA cold-case prosecution in Virginia. "The Gene Squad" aired in 1999, a few months after Dhillon's conviction on December 3, 1998.

Following the Dhillon trial, I decided that one day, when Jessica's killer was finally caught and put away, I was going to write a book, taking that looking-back-at-Carolyn/looking-forward-at-Jessica viewpoint Jerry Thompson and I had originally envisioned for "The Gene Squad." This is that book, a story about those cases and how some good cops did some good police work and hung in until the job was done. While that was happening, a rough-cut forest industry town underwent some major evolutions as it entered the twenty-first century.

Though my long-term goal of writing *The Bulldog and the Helix* dates back to early 1999, by the time I began writing in 2014, I was quite fortunate to have access to a number of critical source materials, many the result of foresight on my part. From my first days at the *Alberni Valley Times*, I saved every story I filed and annotated and stored all of my negatives separately from those of my colleagues. When the *Times* went digital, I saved the images on my hard drive and later transferred them to CDs.

The resulting archive, made up of my own files along with clippings sourced from the *Alberni Valley Times*, the Victoria *Times Colonist*, the *Vancouver Province*, and the *Vancouver Sun* by my *Alberni Valley Times* colleague Denis Houle, provided a clear narrative of the cases as they evolved, and I have striven to attribute these sources in situ. I have also long had an interest in Port Alberni's history, beginning with Jan Peterson's *The Albernis: 1860–1922* and *Twin Cities: Alberni–Port Alberni*. I also have combed through exhibits and writings at the museum. Having that background was invaluable when I began my "accidental" career as a journalist a few years later.

My other main source was the people involved in the cases. As a reporter, there is a temptation to depersonalize tragedy and to treat victims and their families in the abstract. They become "sources," as opposed to genuine human beings in the process of grieving, while at the same time the emotions that are the inevitable result of tragedy are often sought as part of the story. In part because of my own history of childhood trauma, I have always tried to avoid re-traumatizing the people I interview.

In the late 1980s, I became familiar with the issue of post-traumatic stress disorder (PTSD) in first responders during alcohol recovery meetings and listening to the stories of others, including those of first responders. That knowledge provided valuable insight when I began conducting interviews for *The Bulldog and the Helix*, some face to face and some by telephone, all recorded. Listening to the recordings again and hearing the great variation in individual voices led me to tell much of the story in extended quotes to create the effect, for readers, of sitting directly across the table from these investigators and witnesses and hearing their stories first-hand.

Make no mistake, these two crimes have left a lasting impact on the Port Alberni community and beyond. When the subject comes up in conversation, one frequently sees a brief moment of disconnect, a gaze off into the distance that has become a sort of familiar "Oh, that" moment. I had to be conscious of that fact when conducting interviews. Early on, I made the decision not to reach out to families of the aggrieved for interviews though I did contact Rob and Dianne States to advise them about the book and made efforts to locate Carolyn Lee's family.

As I spoke with the people who lived these events, the lingering emotions were telling. Nearly forty years after heading the first stage of the Carolyn Lee investigation, Donald Blair's voice cracked at key moments, in the same way it had during his testimony at the Dhillon trial in 1998. Lyle Price freely admits that the shock of discovering a battered child's body in his potato field still affects him. Again, that is reflected both in his recollections at trial and at lunch at my dining room table. Nearly two decades later, Dan Smith would still slip into a clenched-jaw first-person, present-tense narrative when describing some of the more frustrating moments of the States investigation.

From the very beginning, I wanted to capture that moment when the lab technician identified the DNA profile that led to the arrest of Roderick Patten. As it turned out, Hiron Poon and I graduated from the same Vancouver high school (Sir Winston Churchill Senior Secondary), five years apart, and we had a few of the same teachers. After he provided me with a thorough background on the procedures that were then in use at the RCMP forensic lab, I asked him about the "cold hit." I have striven to share with the reader his bubbly, frenetic description of the next few minutes in that laboratory. Likewise, I wanted the reader to meet the feisty Shelley Arnfield, who earned her place on the Port Alberni General Investigation Section simply by proving she was willing to do what was necessary to get the job done.

Recent innovations in forensic DNA investigation have led to a number of high-profile arrests in murder cases dating all the way back to the 1960s. For Canadians, it all started in Port Alberni, British Columbia, with two terrible tragedies and some dedicated investigators who were willing to push the DNA frontier.

Step Back in Time

MANY OF THE old familiar landmarks have disappeared, but if you want to envision where it all started, back in 1977, take a short hike from what is now Port Alberni's Harbour Quay, a popular destination for tourists at the foot of Argyle Street. In those days, of course, Harbour Quay didn't exist. It wasn't built until the 1980s, when the city undertook a major renovation to make the run-down waterfront more inviting to visitors.

Walk a few blocks past the historic Port Alberni train station and turn left onto Kingsway Avenue. Here, for over a century, the Somass Hotel and its satellite buildings dominated the northeast corner of the intersection before they were demolished in the summer of 2014. A new administrative building and apartment complex owned by Uchucklesaht First Nation now overlooks the waterfront.

Kingsway north of Argyle is an industrial thoroughfare that has not changed much since April 14, 1977, the day twelve-year-old Carolyn Yuen Lee went missing. The marine hardware store has recently expanded into a full-fledged boat dealership, and the tire shop that continues to service the big rigs that haul logs and lumber along the waterfront has undergone some renovations, but the business traffic remains much the same.

On your left are the parking lots that were built for the workforce of the sawmill operated by MacMillan Bloedel's Somass Division, which lies across the railroad tracks. On April 14, 1977, Somass

Division was composed of the A Mill, where the huge old-growth cedar, Douglas fir, and hemlock logs from MacMillan Bloedel's own logging divisions were sliced into lumber and siding; the B Mill, which dated back to the early 1950s, processed smaller logs; and adjacent to this, the shingle mill. In 1977, more than 1,100 workers kept the machinery fed, running three shifts per day.

The Kingsway Hotel still sits at the foot of Athol Street, serving thirsty millworkers since the early days of the Somass Mill although nowadays the clientele is more likely to be retirees. Looking up Athol, the derelict Arrowview Hotel looms over the low cinderblock building known to generations of Port Alberni residents as the Pat Cummings School of Dance, now empty. The hotel was gutted by fire in the spring of 2015 but later purchased for re-development. The city subsequently ordered the building to be demolished, but as of this writing, the building still stands.

With the Arrowview's visibly sagging roof, its fire escapes dangling off the side of the paint-peeled exterior, and its covered-over entryways, one might be tempted to imagine it as a once grand old building only recently fallen on hard times. Maybe it wouldn't have seemed particularly menacing on that spring evening in 1977 when Carolyn Lee left her afternoon dance class and set out on foot toward her family's restaurant, just three and a half blocks away on Third Avenue.

That assumption would be wrong. The story of the Arrowview Hotel in many ways mirrors the fortunes of the forest industry boomtown that spawned it. Built in 1929, the hotel was intended as a drinking establishment, but the city rejected the owner's application for a liquor licence because he already owned the Kingsway Hotel. The required "Men" and "Men and Women" beer parlour entrances had already been roughed in, facing Second Avenue. The owner simply covered them over with plywood, and they remain discernable under successive layers of plywood and particleboard.

Ask a group of long-time Port Alberni residents how the Arrowview subsequently fit into the community, and you will likely receive a variety of responses. Most tellingly, some might not want to comment at all. They might tell you it was a straight-up hotel, and in a sense, they would be right. In 1943, it was taken over by Bloedel, Stewart & Welch Ltd. as a lodging house for single millworkers, and by the 1970s it had been taken over by private owners, who operated a woodworking shop. But if you ask the right person—someone less concerned with maintaining any fiction of gentility—you'll hear the dirty secret: for much of its existence, the Arrowview Hotel was a brothel, where lonely single millworkers and loggers could find temporary female companionship.

MILLTOWN STREETSCAPE

On April 14, 1977, when Carolyn Lee stepped out of the dance school and prepared to walk along Second Avenue to the rear entrance of her parents' restaurant, the Pine Café, Port Alberni still held the distinction of being home to the world's largest wood-processing complex and, through the early 1970s, frequently topped the list of Canadian cities with the highest average annual income. With so much wood processing so close at hand, jobs at the mill or in related support trades were so easy to find that many Port Alberni males dropped out of high school at fifteen or sixteen and within a few months found themselves earning as much as their fathers. They bought the latest muscle cars and partied hard. You could quit a job (or be fired) one day and still be assured of finding another in short order.

In 1967, the CBC aired a thirty-minute documentary, *Young in a Small Town*, focussing on the young generation in Port Alberni and their obsession with the car culture of the day. *Young in a Small Town* painted a picture of circumscribed blue-collar affluence and a seemingly secure future based on the forest industry.

By that last day of Carolyn Lee's short life in 1977, however, cracks were beginning to develop in the local economy. If you were a member of IWA Local 1-85 and you didn't already have a couple of year's seniority locked in, you would eventually fall victim to the massive layoffs that occurred beginning in the early 1980s. If you had stayed out of jail, had not been fired too many times, or had not switched from job to job too recently, you could expect to hold on to your high-paying union job, buy a house and a boat, raise a family, and build up your pension benefits.

But even during the high times, for those who couldn't keep a handle on their lifestyle issues, the picture wasn't so bright. If your work history was spotty, chances are you could be stuck in a shabby rooming house, waiting for the phone to ring. And if you lived at the Arrowview Hotel, chances are you had a good view of the sidewalk in front of the dance school, where the children of your more fortunate co-workers absorbed some of the social graces along with the latest dance steps. The industry collapse was still a few years into the future, but the storm clouds were already gathering on the day Carolyn Lee was abducted, raped, and murdered by a twenty-seven-year-old foundry worker and a still unidentified accomplice. The foundry worker did not have to worry about job security or, as the investigation dragged on, lawyer's fees; his father owned the foundry, which was tucked behind the MacMillan Bloedel's Estevan Division office (since demolished) at the north end of Second Avenue.

LAST SEEN

A photograph of Carolyn Lee and her sister Brenda, taken in front of their home some eighteen blocks east on Argyle Street a short time before Carolyn's disappearance, shows the two of them in a dance pose, arms linked, exuberant. Investigators have never established any link between Carolyn's disappearance and the sketchy rooming house with the clear view of the sidewalk in front of the Pat Cummings School of Dance. But looking east up Athol Street, one might be able to visualize Lee and her fellow students streaming out onto the sidewalk sometime after six o'clock that fateful Thursday. Carolyn, five feet tall and weighing ninety-five pounds, has shoulder-length black hair, and when she leaves the dance school, she is wearing a waist-length navy ski jacket, a sweater with a pale green criss-cross design, blue jeans, and blue runners. She carries a red pull-string tote bag. She and her fellow students joke, they rag each other for mistakes made on the dance floor, they do impromptu dance moves. Some have parents waiting, engines idling.

Setting out from dance class, Carolyn has only three and a half blocks to negotiate, and at the Pine Café, staff are in the middle of the dinnertime rush. Her father, John, usually picks her up at the restaurant at about seven o'clock. So she walks the same way she does every Thursday.

The streetscape she steps into on the last day of her life is noisy and sooty. The streets echo with the sound of pickup trucks and muscle cars roaring up nearby Argyle Street, trying to beat the stoplight at Third Avenue. Just a few blocks away, on the old forty-foot saw carriage at Somass Division A Mill, the head rig noisily bites into giant cedar logs. At the B Mill, smaller logs pass through the gang saw, and at the shingle mill, short chunks of cedar are mechanically slammed back and forth across a razor-sharp splitting blade, trimmed into uniform slabs, and bundled up for sale across North America. And down at the Alberni Foundry, two blocks north, the son of the foundry owner is sharing an end-of-day drink with his father and a few associates before closing up shop and setting out along Second Avenue in his blue Chevy Blazer.

At one time, the Port Alberni waterfront was dotted with giant cone-shaped boilers known as beehive burners, used for burning off the wet waste wood, mostly bark, known as hog fuel. By 1977, MacMillan Bloedel was burning much of that hog fuel to generate electricity for its mills. A large boiler system at Alberni Pacific Division (APD), south of Argyle Street, provided power for both itself and for the Alply plywood mill farther down the shore. APD milled whitewoods, mainly hemlock and balsam fir. The clean chips produced in the milling process were shipped across town to make paper or trucked up to a storage dump located in the hills overlooking the Alberni Inlet.

At Somass Division in 1977, an aboveground conveyor system running along the shoreline transfers wood waste northward to a boiler complex at the sprawling MacMillan Bloedel pulp and paper mill, where two giant concrete smokestacks spew steadily, two twelve-hour shifts per day, seven days a week. Nobody has heard of emission control, and smokestack precipitators will not appear for nearly a decade.

Port Alberni residents still contend with a daily layer of fly ash that settles on every exposed surface overnight.

At each of its big mills, MacMillan Bloedel has installed a rough car wash where workers can hose down the daily layer of grime that accumulates on their brand-new Dodge Chargers and Ford Mustangs and Chevy Camaros while they are on shift cutting logs and moving paper rolls and pulling lumber off the green chain. It's a scene familiar to any kid who lived in a mill town in British Columbia in those days.

IN THE MASSIVE investigation that followed the murder, Port Alberni RCMP soon identified a suspect, but despite some compelling evidence collected at the scene and a credible witness who came forward a few years after the crime, Crown prosecutors didn't have quite enough evidence to lay charges. It would be just five weeks short of twenty years before the foundry owner's son was finally charged.

The Carolyn Lee case would be broken largely through the efforts of one determined member of the RCMP's General Investigation Section (GIS) in Port Alberni who, over the years, immersed himself in the emerging field of forensic DNA investigation and waited for the technology that could process long-degraded crime scene samples to unequivocally link the suspect to the crime scene. Equally important was new federal legislation, enacted on July 13, 1995, which compelled that suspect to provide a DNA sample. While the re-energized Carolyn Lee investigation was unfolding, the community would be rocked by another horrific sex slaying of a pre-teen girl named Jessica States, and the investigator and his colleagues would actively use DNA to track down the killer.

Enter the Bulldog

WHEN RCMP CORPORAL Dan Smith was assigned to the Port Alberni General Investigation Section in January 1988, one of his duties as the "new guy" was to take over old cases still on the books. Photographs of Smith show a medium-tall man with an athletic build, a large jaw, and an easy-going smile. That smile seems to convey the nature of a "nice guy," as his former colleagues describe him, "easy to work with," someone who "liked to stay out of the spotlight."

But look a little closer at those photographs—especially the candid newspaper shots taken of Dan Smith on the job, poring over evidence or speaking at a press conference—and you will notice a characteristic set in the jaw, a reflexive clench in moments of concentration, hinting at a man with deep reserves of focus and determination. You get the impression that, like the legendary bulldog, once this guy sinks his teeth into something, he's not going to let it go. And, as his Port Alberni colleagues discovered, Dan Smith was not a man to let a homicide investigation slip through the bureaucracy—not when it involved the rape and murder of a child.

"The first file I was assigned when I came into General Investigation Section was [the cold-case murder of] Carolyn Lee," Smith said. While he was on record as the lead investigator, he was not expected to conduct an active investigation. "I was assigned the file and told that everything that could be done had been done. This file was given to me simply so I could fill out the C-237." As he discovered, the C-237 was the report that the lead investigator was required to send to head office advising that the investigation was still in progress, no matter how dormant. "You never close down a murder file. This was simply a matter of updating it every six months." Smith was expected to fill out the form even if "there had been no new developments."

While this was his first formal posting with a major crimes unit, Smith already had considerable experience as a street investigator. He arrived in Port Alberni as a General Duty officer in August 1985, after spending most of the first ten years of his career in Prince George, in northern BC.

Smith was born in rural Alberta, but the family moved to Calgary, where he completed his schooling. "In high school, I decided I wanted to be a police officer. I was torn between joining the Calgary Police and the RCMP." For most of its history, the RCMP had a policy of not posting its officers in their home territory, so there was always a tacit understanding that if you joined the force, you could be posted anywhere in Canada except close to home. In those days, the RCMP expected its members to be mobile, and transfers were frequent. In his deliberations, Smith discovered that, while the RCMP had the prestige, the Calgary Police had a higher pay scale. And you didn't have to worry about being posted to some godforsaken corner of Canada.

"You only had to be nineteen to join the RCMP," recalled Smith, "and you had to be twenty to join the Calgary City Police. I applied to the RCMP first, when I was eighteen, and as luck would have it, eleven days after my nineteenth birthday, I found myself in Regina."

Smith entered the RCMP training centre, known as Depot, in 1975. His first posting, in Prince George, was to a booming pulp mill town just in the process of expanding its municipal boundaries. For a rookie Mountie, it was urban policing in a Wild West atmosphere. After just one and a half years, Smith was transferred to Fort Nelson, in the northeast corner of the province, for one year, where the petroleum industry was flourishing. His next posting, again for a single year, was to the forest industry town of Mackenzie. After that, it was 180 kilometres due south on Highway 97, back to Prince George.

For young Mounties, frequent transfers were part of a seasoning process intended both to keep them mobile, but also to provide a range of experience and build up their skill set. And officers who demonstrated specific aptitudes had plenty of opportunity to move up. Smith got that opportunity in Prince George. "I was there from 1979 to 1985, mostly on general duty, but I also spent one year on burglary and one and a half years on court liaison."

"I got to Port Alberni and thought my [dispatch] radio was broken because there were no calls coming in. I never saw any of the other members on my shift, and I always wondered, 'Where did everybody go?' I had come from a place that was three times the size, and the radio traffic was constant. While you were dealing with one call, there were more calls backing up for you."

When Smith came to the General Investigation Section in Port Alberni in early 1988, the unit was commanded by Sergeant Murray Sawatsky. He'd earned a reputation as a top-notch investigator who supported his team members and let them take credit when credit was due. When a GIS slot came open, he invited Smith to come on board.

As a new investigator, Smith had a case file in his hand, albeit one that was more than ten years old. While the murder of Carolyn Lee was still fresh in the minds of the people of Port Alberni, RCMP members tended to move frequently, and the case was not uppermost in the minds of local officers by 1988. "I knew it had happened, but I was not privy to the details ... I knew it had not been solved."

A cursory examination of the file revealed that a suspect had been identified shortly after the killing, but investigators were unable to put together a case against him. On November 26, 1983, the suspect's ex-wife had given police a statement that strongly indicated his guilt, but again, there just wasn't enough evidence to take to court. In July 1984, the suspect had been charged in a pair of unrelated sexual assault cases but was later acquitted. While he was known to local police, he didn't stand out.

"He wasn't really on our radar, as far as keeping an eye on him. There were far more active criminals I dealt with on a daily basis. I was probably aware of him, but that was about the extent of it ... until, of course, I got conduct of the file."

By now, the Carolyn Lee investigation had generated a full filing cabinet of evidence, investigation reports, press clippings, and sundry paperwork. Surely, Smith believed, there must be something in there that held the key to solving this case. The easy thing to do would have been to simply follow instructions and dutifully fill out the C-237 report every six months to say the investigation was still open but that there was nothing new to report. "However, as luck would have it, as I was new to the Major Crimes Unit, and I didn't yet have a whole lot on my plate, I undertook a file review."

For Dan Smith, it was the beginning of a nine-year journey to bring a murder charge against the man who had been the prime suspect since the earliest days of the investigation. During that time, the infant science of forensic DNA would evolve into the most potent new weapon in the hands of police investigators since the fingerprint, and the Carolyn Lee prosecution would have to ride the outer edge of the available technology and law until the final guilty verdict came down in December 1998.

DISAPPEARED

In Port Alberni, people subscribe to the philosophy, "If you don't like the weather, wait five minutes." The changeability of west coast weather just might have played a major role in the life and death of Carolyn Lee. On April 14, 1977, when Carolyn and her classmates at the Pat Cummings School of Dance wrapped up their Thursday afternoon tap dance session and stepped out onto the sidewalk on Athol Street, west of Second Avenue, just before 6:30 PM, the early evening air was pleasant but cool, appropriate for the winter coat Carolyn wore. The sun would soon dip behind Cataract Mountain on the west shore of the harbour, but it was still daylight.

Just as Carolyn prepared to leave, Pat Cummings leaned out the front door to remind her that she was required to acquire a leotard or a body suit for the upcoming year-end performance. "Carolyn, Carolyn. Don't forget to order your suit from the catalogue," she called out.

Nancy Moore, also twelve, was waiting outside for a ride from her brother. Twenty-one years later, she testified that Carolyn had just begun the short walk along Second Avenue to the Pine Café when her brother drove up. "He asked her if she wanted a ride, and she said no, she'd rather walk."

Would Carolyn have accepted a ride from Nancy's brother if it had been raining? In her waist-length ski jacket, she was prepared for the unpredictable spring weather, and it was only a short walk to the Pine Café. Furthermore, Carolyn's father, John Lee, would later say that he had cautioned his daughter "very explicitly not to accept rides at all." John concluded that two people must have been involved, and that Carolyn was abducted by force. Investigators had already come to that conclusion. Had the young dancer accepted that ride with Nancy's brother, she might well have been alive today.

On Second Avenue, Carolyn crossed paths with another dancer, Janice Pierce, fourteen, who was on her way to a seven o'clock ballet class. They exchanged a brief "Hi" in passing. Janice was the last person to positively report seeing Carolyn alive.

According to Carolyn's older sister, Linda, Carolyn would normally arrive at the restaurant after dance class, at about 6:45, and her father would drive from their home at the top of Argyle Street to pick her up. But when he arrived that evening, Carolyn had not shown up as expected. John Lee then drove the short distance to the dance school only to find she wasn't there either. At this point, he drove to the Port Alberni Gymnastics Academy to pick up Carolyn's sister Brenda and then drove home, where he started to make phone calls. At eight o'clock, he contacted local RCMP. Before the first hour was out, police had begun a search along Carolyn's walking route and gradually expanded the search area to include nearby local parks.

Sergeant Donald Blair, head of the Port Alberni GIS, was at home when watch commander John Fox contacted him at 9:00 PM to tell him that a twelve-year-old girl was missing. Blair immediately assumed command of the search.

"It sounded serious enough that I went down to the office and we carried on from there," Blair said. "I think her age had a lot to do with it. If she was sixteen, we might have said, 'If she's not back by noon tomorrow, give us a call.' But we were concerned right off the bat." There had been instances when girls went missing, but the circumstances surrounding this situation felt different. "In those days, if a teenage girl didn't come home, they usually had trouble at home or they had trouble somewhere else. About ninety percent of the time, that's what the situation was, and that's why police wouldn't get fired up right away."

But this was no sexualized high school kid; this was a pre-teen girl from a well-known, hard-working Chinese family, walking a familiar three-and-a-half block route in broad daylight. And that set off all the alarm bells. Carolyn's sister Linda later told the *Alberni Valley Times* that, at the time of her murder, Carolyn "didn't look a day over her twelve years. Carolyn was just a child," she said. "She looked and acted like one. She didn't look older than she was, and she wasn't even interested in boys."

Instilling a sense of responsibility was a priority in the Lee family. John and his wife Sau Kuen routinely put in long hours at the restaurant, which meant the children were required to supervise themselves at home. Being the eldest, Linda frequently took charge. She characterized Carolyn as a quiet girl who succeeded at almost everything she attempted, as well as being a good athlete. "She never picked fights. In fact, she was the type that people took advantage of, she was so easy-going. Even at home, if there was something that had to be done, and no one wanted to do it, Carolyn would do it. She didn't complain about anything. Nobody would ever have a grudge against her."

THE SEARCH

That night, as Carolyn's half-clothed body lay on the muddy shore of a small lake south of the city, snow fell, adding to the mud of spring. The hastily assembled team of searchers combed the Alberni Valley overnight and into the next day, working in difficult conditions.

The Alberni Valley Rescue Squad was a group of volunteers trained and equipped for the sort of search and rescue operations one might expect in an industrial community surrounded by water and forests and mountains. They might be called out to locate a missing hiker on nearby Mount Arrowsmith or to rope-rescue anyone foolish enough to try paddling through Stamp Falls Gorge. But the Rescue Squad was about to enter a new phase. Within a few minutes of arriving at the detachment and assessing the situation, Sergeant Blair became convinced that he was dealing with a kidnapping and that he needed to get as many bodies and as many search vehicles on the street as possible as quickly as possible because Carolyn might be lying injured on the side of a road somewhere—and minutes counted.

For the volunteers, this wasn't a search for an overdue fisherman or a missing hunter—they would be searching for a victim of crime with the suspect or suspects still at large. Members of the local CB radio club set up a base to coordinate communications between rescue vehicles and police, and the Rescue Squad teams took to the streets, beginning with Carolyn's Second Avenue walking route, then gradually expanding into the Third Avenue business district and the waterfront.

The local radio station, CJAV 1240, issued bulletins with a description of Carolyn and urged residents to check their own properties for any sign of the missing girl. The next morning, police brought in a tracking dog from Vancouver and an RCMP helicopter from Victoria. By then, it seemed certain that this was, in fact, a kidnapping.

At Port Alberni's West Coast General Hospital, staff members were alerted to watch for people with suspicious injuries. Dry-cleaners were contacted to keep an eye out for bloody clothes. City garbage collectors were alerted to watch for unusual items on their pickup routes. Probation officers were canvassed about clients, and even psychiatrists were approached for any hint of suspicion that a client might be involved.

At Maquinna Elementary School, teachers and classmates were grilled about Carolyn's activities and her behaviour. Was she depressed?

Did anyone know if she had run away from home? According to all sources, Carolyn was behaving normally. In the Friday, April 15, edition of the *Alberni Valley Times*, the headline announced "12-Year-Old Girl Missing." (The *Times* erroneously spelled her name "Caroline" in the story and in the photo caption.)

The *Times* came out every afternoon. That day, when the *Times* sent the pages to press at noon, the search operation was still active, so the story included a description of Carolyn and urged readers to contact police if they had any information on her whereabouts. By the time most readers picked up the paper at dinnertime, the operation was just shifting from an active missing-person search to a crime scene investigation.

INITIAL INVESTIGATION

The morning of April 15, RCMP and Rescue Squad members had been combing the Alberni Valley for nineteen straight hours when the watch commander contacted Sergeant Blair to advise that "the missing girl had been discovered." Her body was found near Cox Lake, about four kilometres south from the southwestern edge of town, off Franklin River Road. To get there from the dance studio, a driver would have two options to reach Ship Creek Road, which linked up with Franklin River Road. The shortest but most exposed route would require the suspect vehicle to take busy Third Avenue. Heading south on Third Avenue, a driver could make a hard right down the hill toward the sawmill, ease right onto Plywood Road to the plywood mill, or continue a half block further south and swing left onto Ship Creek Road.

For the alternative route, the driver would go west a short distance to the bottom of Argyle Street and turn left onto Harbour Road, travel along the waterfront to the entrance of the sawmill, and then east up South Street to the Ship Creek Road junction at Third Avenue. The waterfront route, which flanked the rail line that brought lumber to the Assembly Wharf, swung left at the mill and back up to Third Avenue. It was a considerably longer route, but it would have exposed the suspect vehicle to less pedestrian and vehicle traffic.

Ship Creek Road had been built only recently, at MacMillan Bloedel's expense, to provide a truck route from the mill to the chip dump off Sezai Road. Ship Creek crosses the city limits at Anderson Avenue and becomes Franklin River Road, which, in 1977, was still unpaved. Today, the entire stretch is seamlessly paved past Cox Lake, all the way to a junction at the City of Port Alberni chlorination station, which was installed in the 1960s. At the junction, a driver might swing left up the Cameron Main logging road toward Mount Arrowsmith or turn right and continue along Franklin River Road.

From 1912 through 1957, the Alberni Valley was criss-crossed with rail lines, operated by a variety of companies, for extracting and hauling logs to the hodgepodge of mills that sprang up and disappeared over that period. By 1977, forest companies had converted entirely to truck logging; the railway tracks had been pulled and the steam locomotives hauled away to be resurrected decades later as tourist attractions. Some of the old railbeds and spur lines had been repurposed as roads, but in many instances, their remnants remained visible.

One such old railbed ran by Lyle Price's potato fields. That Friday morning, the fields were covered with a thin wet blanket of snow. Twenty-nine-year-old Price co-owned and operated Port Potato, a farm located at 725 Franklin River Road, past Cox Lake and just short of the junction at the chlorination station. It would be weeks before he could put in his seed potatoes. Price had to run into town that morning with a truckload of potatoes from last year's crop.

"It had been a miserable night, and my oldest kid was sick with the flu. We were up most of the night with him," Price recalled, thirty-seven years later. "We had just gotten to bed with him, and we hadn't gotten much sleep. Then, about one o'clock in the morning, my Labrador, Jake, started to growl, and he kept it up till about four. That was completely out of character for him."

Had it been a deer or a bear, Price says, Jake would have simply chased it out of the yard. Despite the official timeline, which put the suspects at Cox Lake just minutes after Carolyn's abduction, Price still has his doubts about the prosecution's version of events, based on Jake's behaviour during the night of the killing. "My dog said they drove in there at one in the morning," he said. "He had never in his whole life growled like that, and never did afterward."

Price got up at about 7:30 that morning and made his delivery run into Port Alberni. He returned later in the morning and did some chores in the potato warehouse before his wife Jackie called him to lunch. It was the first he had heard about the search for Carolyn.

"My wife said, 'I was just listening to the radio, and there's a girl missing in town. They're asking people to check their rural properties.'" That stirred a growing realization. Price had seen members of the Alberni Valley Rescue Squad at the edge of Franklin River Road, but they hadn't come onto his property. He was still processing it when Jackie set the hook. "She said, 'Remember how Jake was last night? Why don't you get your bike out and have a look around.'"

For years, Price said, he remembered taking Jackie's suggestion and immediately launching a search of the farm on his dirt bike. But he concedes now that there must have been a gap of a few hours from lunchtime to when he started his actual search. Most likely, he believes, he completed a few more routine tasks before firing up the motorcycle. After making a few sweeps in different directions across the property, Price then sped down a short section of the old Weist Logging/Alberni Pacific Lumber Company railbed that ran past his house toward Cox Lake, a distance of about seven hundred metres. Close to the lake, a railway spur line cut into the main line at an angle of approximately 130 degrees, requiring any vehicle to make an extremely tight (and blind) right-hand turn. The spur line ran about 120 metres back to an abandoned landing that lay parallel to Franklin River Road, just below the roadway. At the junction, Price hit the brakes and came to a sudden stop.

"There was a fresh set of tire tracks there. And I got a very bad feeling at that point," he said. It was obvious to Price that the vehicle had been a four-wheel drive with heavy-duty traction tires because of the tread patterns and the fact that it hadn't slipped in the muddy roadway. "The tire tracks came down it and made that turn without backing up or anything. Whoever went in there knew that road was there and had been there before."

With a sinking feeling, Price shut the bike down and began to walk up the spur, carefully staying between the tire tracks in the mud. After following the path for a hundred metres, he stopped. About twenty metres ahead, lying in front of the old landing, was the half-naked body of a young girl. "I got close enough to realize that she was deceased," he said.

Years later, Price recalls that he had the presence of mind to avoid contaminating the crime scene by rushing and in touching the body or leaving footprints all over the place. Now mindful that the entire area was an active crime scene, Price carefully backtracked to the junction and retrieved his motorcycle. Realizing that he was closer to his neighbour's home than his own, he drove straight to the Murray farm to contact police. Price told Mrs. Murray that he had found the missing girl. He called the RCMP and told them he would show them where the body was located.

In a show of force, detachment commander, Inspector Bob Stitt, joined Sergeant Blair and his team at the crime scene. "We parked at Franklin River Road and the junction into Cox Lake," Blair said. "We left our vehicles there and walked in, just so we could preserve anything that was there."

Blair and his team found Carolyn lying on her left side, wearing only her ski jacket and her sneakers. A quick examination led them to believe she had died of head injuries. Investigators found the rest of her clothes scattered along a nearby path.

The question of where the assault took place and whether the Cox Lake site was merely where her body was dumped has never been fully settled. Investigators found no obvious signs of struggle at the scene, and had Price not specifically conducted a search of the property, Carolyn's body may not have been found for weeks or months. Blair believed that for a murderer with a body to dispose of, it might have looked like a quick and easy solution—but he had to know the area.

"We worked into the night," recalled Blair, "and left a member at the crime scene overnight. The Ident guys came in first thing the next morning and made casts of the [tire] tracks. I don't remember any snow on the ground when we got to the crime scene, but it was muddy, and that was fortunate, because it made for clear impressions."

Over the next several days, police performed an extensive search of the entire area. "We got all our auxiliaries out and walked the Cox Lake bush from between where the body was found and Franklin River Road and right down to the lake. We basically joined hands and covered that whole property because we were looking for some sort of a weapon that he had used to hit her on the head with," Blair said. They also collected and preserved a great deal of evidence, including a set of five vaginal swabs from Carolyn's body and various soil samples from the crime scene. A sample of grit taken from a footprint on the back of Carolyn's jacket would later prove critical in reopening the investigation.

Dog teams tracked down scents, and a dive team waded the muddy shoreline of Cox Lake looking for a weapon or anything of interest. But on that first day, after telling his wife and fending off the initial waves of horror and dread, Price discovered one of the hard truths of police work: if you discover the body of a murder victim, you are automatically the first suspect—until someone better comes along.

The RCMP called him at home that night, telling him he was required to come to the Sixth Avenue detachment "to answer some questions." When Price arrived, he was escorted to a small room. It didn't feel right. "I realized this was the interrogation room. They started to ask questions, and I gave them the details as I knew them. And they started grilling me pretty good."

After pushing the interrogation for a few more minutes, the officer in charge then demanded that Price undergo a lie detector test. Price realized the interrogators were swerving outside the lines of strict police procedure on the off chance he might reveal something voluntarily. And he wasn't having any part of it. "I said, 'Look—I've just been through something pretty traumatic. You can take your test and shove it.' I said, 'You want to know where I was last night, phone my wife.'"

The next day, Saturday, April 16, the RCMP called him back in for another interview. The approach was softer, but still didn't ring true. "This time, they said, 'Don't say anything to anybody.'" Price angrily assured police he wasn't going to speak about his discovery of a murder scene. He had not spoken to reporters, and the RCMP assured him they had not released his name.

The *Alberni Valley Times* would not publish their story, which referred to Price only as "a local resident," until Monday, June 18. But that night, his phone started to ring. First it was the CBC, looking for comment, then the newspapers. Thirty-seven years later, his resentment was still palpable. "I was really pissed that they had released my name. I know the only place they could have got it from was the RCMP."

The investigators lost interest in Price as a suspect soon enough, but they did contact him occasionally during the ongoing investigation, usually for information about the physical layout of the farm or for local information. Sergeant Blair didn't take part in the questioning, nor did he meet Price at the time of the investigation. "We didn't really consider him any kind of a suspect," Blair said. "But that request [to interview him] came from upstairs. That's why we had to put the pressure on, to go through the process to satisfy the powers that be. I remember he was quite offended."

Price said he had the impression that the murder weapon was a wooden object, because RCMP divers spent several days combing Cox Lake, looking for something that may have been thrown into the lake and later washed ashore. Price told the divers that they were looking at the wrong end of the lake, based on his observation of the flooding that took place each winter. Rather than floating to the outfall at the lower end of the lake, he advised them, any floating debris would, due to the prevailing winds, accumulate at the higher end.

"Nobody ever told me what killed her, but they did ask me where something wooden would end up," he said. Sergeant Blair, however, said he didn't recall anything specifically that indicated the murder weapon was wooden. "We were just looking for anything that could have been used."

Price subsequently reported one very strange and disturbing incident that took place a year later, almost on the anniversary of the crime. "It was about two o'clock in the morning. A vehicle came down our driveway and did a circle in the bottom of the driveway and drove out again. It was in the middle of the night. I got up. It woke me up because the dog barked. I looked out, and it was a frickin' blue Blazer, and I'm sure it was an East Indian driving it." At the time, however, Price had no idea that the RCMP had long established a suspect of Indo-Canadian descent who owned a blue Blazer.

IT WAS THE tire tracks that led investigators to Gurmit Singh Dhillon, who at that time lived at 2595 Second Avenue with his common-law wife, Sharon McLeod, and her children. Investigators consulted local tire dealers to determine the type of tires involved. Pearson Tire was located kitty-corner to the foundry across Third Avenue, while Jack's Tires was barely a block away on Kingsway. Owners Earl Pearson and Jack Mackenzie both concluded that the suspect's vehicle was mounted with four 700 x 15 Seiberling commuter lug tires, typically used on four-wheel-drive trucks.

From there it was a matter of getting enough investigators out on the street. The city was divided up into four zones, with a corporal in charge of each zone, and three or four patrol officers in each squad. The first target was parking lots. With so many men employed in shifts at the big MacMillan Bloedel operations, this tactic was expected to locate the suspect's vehicle relatively quickly—provided he was a forest industry worker. Each officer carried a photograph of the tire tracks and knew to look for a four-wheel drive.

Blair said one factor working in their favour was that investigators were sure the suspect was a local person. When Carolyn Lee's body was first discovered, he explained, everybody was a suspect. Then, once it could be proved that a specific vehicle was involved, that narrowed down the focus. "But we knew it must be a local person, because, if you're not a local person, you wouldn't know that road into Cox Lake was there."

When parking lots failed to yield a matching truck, the search shifted to residences in the same zones. It was a combination of leads that led investigators to Dhillon's driveway at the corner of Second Avenue and Bruce. On April 25, ten days after the body was discovered, Constable Ian MacDonald was assigned to investigate a claim by an Indigenous woman named Mildred Rose Mickey that, some time prior to the murder, she had been driven to the same wooded area near Cox Lake and indecently assaulted.

With investigators already searching residential areas as part of the Lee investigation, MacDonald decided to drive Mickey through some of the neighbourhoods in town. When she spotted a blue 1977 Blazer in Dhillon's driveway, she recognized it right away. Mickey told MacDonald it looked exactly like the truck driven by her assailant.

Looking back, Blair said Mickey's identification of the suspect's vehicle was a real break. "There was nothing whatsoever pointing us towards Dhillon. We were just checking for tires, and he [MacDonald] was fortunate enough to drive her down that street."

Without probable cause to question the owner, MacDonald had to settle for a discreet inspection of the tires on the Blazer. All four tires were of the same heavy-duty traction tread, made by Seiberling. The size, 700 x 15, matched the specifications provided by Earl Pearson and Jack Mackenzie. For the past week, every patrol officer in Port Alberni had been carrying photographs of the tire impressions taken at the crime scene by the Ident unit. When MacDonald held up the photograph to the tires on the Blazer, it was a perfect match. After running the plates, MacDonald took Mickey back to the detachment to see if she could identify the suspect. Because Dhillon already had a police record, his picture was on file.

Leafing through a series of police photographs, Mickey breezed right past Dhillon. When MacDonald risked pointing out Dhillon's image, she was quick to dismiss it. "That's not him," she said. "He [the man she saw] isn't a Hindu [Indo-Canadian]."

Twenty-one years later, Dhillon's defence counsel grilled MacDonald at trial, contending that the investigator had violated his integrity as a police officer by pointing out Dhillon's image. But whether his actions constituted a breach of police policy in those pre-Charter of Rights and Freedoms times or not, they had categorically eliminated half the case against Gurmit Singh Dhillon. On the other hand, investigators still had the tire tracks, and they led straight to the foundry owner's son.

On the Monday that MacDonald and Mickey identified Dhillon's Blazer as the suspect vehicle, the *Alberni Valley Times* published an update on the story under the headline "Investigation Help Sought." With Sergeant Blair as the source, it announced that no new leads had been reported although "questioning of people in town and a ground search of the area" continued. At this point, Blair wanted to find out just how many people knew about the Cox Lake spur road and how travelled it was. "Police say no weapon was found by divers searching muddy Cox Lake," the report continued. Blair told the *Times* that he particularly wanted "to hear from youths who frequently visited the area for drinking parties, girls who were driven there by their boyfriends, or fishermen who visited the spots."

Blair also reported that, in the course of the ongoing investigation, the RCMP had learned of "several sex-related offences that occurred up to two years ago," likely referring to the Mickey assault. "[The] RCMP have no plans to lay charges in connection with old sexual offences that surface during the course of their investigation," Blair concluded.

Having staked out the ground rules in the *Times* concerning unconnected sexual offences, Blair went to the Alberni Foundry the following day to take a statement from Dhillon. Blair had been careful not to reveal that police had a suspect in their sights—what he had was a guy whose tire tracks matched impressions taken at the crime scene, and that was it. "That's why we didn't advertise that we were looking for someone with Seiberling tires, because they wouldn't last too long. Anyone with any sense would either get rid of them or call us up and say, 'I've got those tires. I wasn't there.'" Blair knew he needed more than a plaster cast to make an arrest. "What we needed was that one piece of evidence that would put Carolyn in that truck."

Mickey had positively identified the blue Blazer, but emphatically excluded the owner as her assailant. Blair and MacDonald subsequently drove Mickey out to the Cox Lake area to see if she could identify the site where her assault had taken place. Blair said she did not react when they drove past the spur line where Carolyn's body was found. Mickey only expressed a vague familiarity with a couple of derelict vehicles in the general area. That didn't give Blair a lot of leverage with which to confront a murder suspect.

"When I interviewed Dhillon, I knew he would have an alibi, which is fine. All I wanted to do was get the alibi down, and then what you do is try to disprove it. I wanted to get out of him that nobody borrowed his truck that evening; that was the big thing."

Faced with direct questions from the lead RCMP investigator, Dhillon made no attempt to implicate any associate. On the evening of April 14, he told Blair, he had stayed at the foundry until sometime between 6:30 and 7:00 PM, drinking with his father, two brothers, and a couple of customers. This was fairly normal activity at the foundry, he maintained.

After locking up, Dhillon, as was his practice, drove straight out of the foundry parking lot to the Somass Division car wash and had the Blazer hosed down. After that, he told Blair, he drove straight to the Beaufort Hotel, located at Third Avenue and Mar, just two blocks south of Argyle. According to his statement, Dhillon went into the beer parlour and ordered two beers. He saw one acquaintance, Don McMurtry, and spoke to the bartender, Ken Sherman. He called McLeod at home, was unable to reach her, and then ordered two more beer. Later, while he drank, McLeod called the hotel, looking for him. Dhillon said he left the bar at 8:30 and that McLeod was angrily waiting for him outside. She then followed him home, a drive of just seven blocks, in her car. Perhaps significantly, however, they did confirm that he was familiar with the road into Cox Lake. "We used to drink there as kids," he told Blair.

After giving his statement, Dhillon turned over his Blazer to the investigators for several hours. They searched the vehicle thoroughly, took fingerprints, and vacuumed up all manner of soil, particles, and fibres, and sent everything off to the Crime Detection Laboratory in Vancouver. It was now July 15, three months after Carolyn's murder.

"We also took the vacuum cleaner bag out of their home because, if he had gone home and vacuumed out his car, we might find something," Blair said. "I even took him down to Victoria for a polygraph. I was surprised he agreed. But at the time, they said the results were inconclusive."

The next year, Sergeant Blair transferred out to take over as detachment commander in Fort Nelson in northeastern BC. He said it was difficult to leave Port Alberni with the Carolyn Lee case unsolved. "Things were pretty much stalled. We were pretty sure we had the right guy, but then we got the polygraph results, and we weren't so sure," he said. "But I'm quite thoroughly convinced we did a reasonably good job with the resources we had available. Nowadays, with this type of case, they wheel in a command post and a dozen senior guys. In those days, it fell to the local members, with some outside help, such as the helicopter and the dive team that came in. Would [the investigation] have been more efficient if [the crime] had happened years later? Who knows? I can't see that we made any mistakes, but we didn't get any really big breaks, either."

While Dhillon had emerged as the main suspect, investigators interviewed all known sex offenders and even asked employers to identify employees who were absent from work on the afternoon of the abduction. Each was subsequently interviewed. Employers were also asked to provide the names of any men who were in town looking for work, and investigators scrutinized the guest lists of all local hotels and motels.

As Dan Smith continued to review the Lee case files, he noted that Blair's replacement at the Port Alberni GIS, Sergeant Bob Martin, would be at the helm when the Carolyn Lee investigation moved into its next, equally frustrating phase, when Dhillon was to be charged in two unrelated sexual assault complaints and when his ex-wife made a statement to police. Now, eleven years after the crime and confronted with a mountain of paperwork in the case file, Dan Smith continued to look for something to re-energize the investigation.

"There was just no chance of reading everything in the file. They were just sequential papers, filed starting on day one," he said. The files had not been collated or organized by topic or by the names of the witnesses interviewed. They had merely been entered in the order they were received, then stamped and dated. Smith knew if he was going to find a game-changer, it was not going to jump out of the mass of documents accumulated in the Carolyn Lee file cabinet.

"But there was one exception, and that was the exhibits that were seized and the lab analysis. They were two separate sub-files." Of particular interest was the vacuum cleaner bag that had been used when examining the Blazer. Perhaps there was something in that bag, some trace material, that had not been detected in the 1977 lab analysis. Perhaps there was some new forensic process that had come along in the past decade.

ON APRIL 18, 1977, three days after Carolyn Lee's body was found, Dorothy Clark, an analyst in the hair and fibre section of the forensic lab in Vancouver, received a number of exhibits, including items of Carolyn Lee's clothing and samples of her hair (head and pubic). Later Clark was sent Dhillon's hair samples (head and pubic). She subsequently concluded that a pubic hair found on Carolyn's sweater belonged to neither the victim nor the suspect. Similarly, a number of scalp hairs found on her clothing were also foreign to both. They were described as "light in colouring and Caucasian in origin."

Clark also examined a footprint left on Carolyn's jacket. The impression was of a Vibram sole typical of a work boot. While the impression was insufficient to identify a specific boot, the granular residue left in the footprint was to prove critical in restarting the investigation. Clark's colleague, serologist David O'Keefe, received the swabs taken from the victim (Exhibits 21 and 24). On May 3, he would receive the clothing items first examined by his hair and fibre analyst colleague. O'Keefe was able to identify human semen and spermatozoa in Exhibit 21. All exhibits were analyzed for the presence of blood, and all proved negative, except for one soil sample and the jacket. Both samples were consistent with the victim's blood.

Three months later, Clark received two vacuum cleaner bags and their contents. One had been collected at the Dhillon home on April 26, and the other was taken from Dhillon's Blazer on the same day. Clark examined the human scalp hair found in both vacuum bags but was unable to find any scalp or pubic hairs that matched the victim. The presence of pubic and scalp hairs unrelated to the victim or the accused suggested that there was a second, Caucasian suspect involved in the assault and killing. Over the next twelve years, two suspects would emerge, and there were sufficient grounds to obtain hair samples from the two, who were identified only by initials.

In August 1981, hair and fibre analyst Julian Ann Graham received scalp and pubic hair samples taken from one individual, PRK. Graham compared them to the pubic hair found on Carolyn Lee's sweater and scalp hairs found on her leotards, ski jacket, and a blanket and subsequently concluded that PRK's known hairs were not consistent with the questioned hairs. In November 1989, after Dan Smith inherited the case, Graham would reach a similar conclusion following examination of known hair samples collected from another individual, TG.

NEW WITNESS STATEMENT

Continuing through the files, Dan Smith discovered that Dhillon's partner, Sharon McLeod, had made a statement to police on November 23, 1983, fully six years after the crime, following her separation from Dhillon. On November 16, 1998, she testified that, when investigators first came to her home to talk to Dhillon, she didn't pay much attention. Later, when the RCMP arrived with a search warrant, she was home alone. She told the court that she had stood outside the home while investigators conducted the search, and in fact, police never interviewed her.

When McLeod married Dhillon in 1981, she was well aware that he was still a person of interest in the killing of Carolyn Lee, and she knew he was "a drinker and a womanizer," but she didn't believe the police accusation that he was a murderer. "Looking back," Blair said in hindsight, "I'm pretty convinced that if we had interviewed her, she wouldn't have given us anything."

But in 1983, McLeod told Sergeant Bob Martin that, on the night of the killing, she made dinner at six and waited for Dhillon to come home from work. When he didn't show up by 6:30, she drove down to the foundry to see if he was still there. When she saw the foundry was locked up for the night, she "tried a few nearby bars" but was unable to locate him, and she returned home within fifteen minutes. She told police that she then phoned "a few bars" but couldn't remember specifically calling the Beaufort Hotel, where Dhillon told Blair he'd been.

McLeod's testimony at the trial in 1998, if it is accurate, suggests that Dhillon chose the most exposed route out of town, turning onto Third Avenue at the edge of the uptown business district with a captive twelve-year-old girl in the back seat. She had told police that, at about 7:00 PM, she was looking out her east-facing kitchen window when she saw Dhillon pass by in the Blazer, heading south toward the Ship Creek Road junction. This had not been part of her original statement in 1983. From their house on the corner of Bruce Street and Second Avenue, she would have a reasonably good view of the intersection at Third Avenue. When Dhillon did not make the right turn onto Bruce, McLeod said she assumed he had driven one block further to Anne's Grocery to buy cigarettes. He didn't get home until 7:30.

While Dhillon told Blair that he'd run his Blazer through the free car wash at Somass Division, according to McLeod, when he returned home that night, the vehicle was caked with mud and the wheel wells were jammed with sticks and brush. Dhillon was "not friendly," and he demanded that she wash the truck. Sergeant Blair said the Blazer was clean when his crew went through it on April 26. Had Dhillon driven the vehicle on the Cox Lake dirt road, it would have needed more than a quick pass through the car wash to get rid of the mud. "I went through that car wash many times in police cars," said Blair. "All it did was knock the dust off the roof and sides. It didn't spray under the car or blast out the wheel wells." The Blazer had definitely been washed by hand, and the wheel wells and undercarriage were clean when police examined the vehicle.

McLeod later testified that she frequently washed Dhillon's truck by hand, and that on the night of the murder, the mud on the truck did not look like dirt from the foundry. She thought he must have been out four-wheeling in the short interval between when she saw him drive by at about seven and half an hour later when he pulled into the driveway, acting surly. McLeod told police she'd found a blue, bow-shaped barrette and an earring with a wire hook in the Blazer that night, but neither, on further investigation, had belonged Carolyn Lee.

While investigators sought to put together a solid case against Dhillon based on McLeod's statement in 1983, the suspect found himself implicated in a pair of unrelated sexual assaults involving adult women. As a result of one of the complaints, which alleged that on February 12, 1984, Dhillon had assaulted a fifty-four-year-old woman, he was charged with one count of sexual assault and one count of buggery under the Criminal Code of the day. Dhillon was not formally charged until July 3, however. By that time, he had been taken into custody as a result of another sexual assault allegation filed on June 28 by a thirty-six-year-old woman. Dhillon was charged on both complaints and was set to appear for a preliminary hearing on August 3, 1984.

BUT THE DHILLON investigation had not gone unnoticed in the community. In an unsourced article on April 19, boxed under a headline "No Arrest in Murder," Port Alberni RCMP told the public there was no arrest in sight for the Carolyn Lee murder. "The streets are ripe with rumours, the police confirmed, but the *Times* was told, 'there is no evidence to make an arrest.'"

According to the "rumours," it was widely understood that Dhillon was a prime suspect in the investigation, and the first set of assault allegations had raised hopes that the case, now seven years old, would be broken. What was not mentioned was that, shortly after Sharon McLeod made her statement to police, Dhillon submitted to a second polygraph test, which was again determined to be "inconclusive." But by April, the RCMP had decided to quash expectations.

"The *Times* story is prompted by the public concern in the latest series of rumours and is published in the interest of quieting inaccurate speculation that is alive in the community and not fuelling more," the article concluded. In hopes of encouraging any previously reluctant witnesses to come forward, the Carolyn Lee Memorial Committee reissued the reward it had offered at the time of the crime. The newly reissued reward totalled $11,000 and was valid through May 31, 1985. In the *Times*, Carolyn Lee Memorial Committee spokesman Ramon (Ray) Kwok observed: "There has been a lot of talk around town about what is happening," adding his hopes that the reward might encourage someone to come forward with more information.

THE FOOTPRINT

Despite the statement from Dhillon's estranged wife and the wave of rumours it generated—enough to trigger the re-issuing of the reward—the Crown was not satisfied that it had enough evidence to make a case, especially after the 1984 sexual assault charges were dismissed by the court. But when looking through the lab analysis reports, Smith believed he had found a window to reopen the investigation. Reviewing the case, Smith knew that Dhillon was considered a "strong subject of interest" who'd originally been eliminated through polygraph examination. Later, however, the polygraph results had been re-examined and deemed "inconclusive." Dhillon had tires on his vehicle that were the same size, shape, and tread pattern as the ones that made the tracks at the crime scene.

But what stuck in Smith's mind was the fact that Dhillon worked in a foundry. Smith, who had schooled himself in the making of firearms and ammunition, including the working and casting of metals, was convinced that Dhillon must have left trace materials at the crime scene that were unique to a working foundry. "I was wondering if metals that were common in a foundry could be found in the footprint that was left on the back of Carolyn's jacket. The suspect, when he killed her, stepped on the back of her jacket."

Going through the records from the forensic lab in Vancouver, Smith discovered that the soil sample had not been analyzed specifically for metal content. Back in 1977, the RCMP chemist, Brian Richardson, had analyzed the soil samples, and while he did not look for nor analyze any metal content, he did reach several salient conclusions. First, the soil found in the footprint (Exhibit 18) contained "one small spherical particle that appeared to be metal." The soil from the jacket was of a different composition from the soil underneath the victim's body and the soil from the nearby roadside. And none of the soil samples except Exhibit 18 contained any spherical objects.

Smith discovered that there was still an uncontaminated sample of the footprint soil among the physical exhibits. As he transitioned into his new role in the Port Alberni GIS, Smith waited for an opportunity to find out whether there were any trace metals in the fatal footprint that were specific to a foundry. He telephoned analyst Tony Fung at the Vancouver lab and explained that he wanted a detailed spectrographic analysis of soil in relation to an unsolved eleven-year-old murder investigation in Port Alberni, specifically to identify cast-off metals from a foundry.

Fung said the best he could do was to compare the soil from the footprint with a sample of soil taken from the foundry. There were two problems with that suggestion. First, eleven years had elapsed since the crime, and unless Alberni Foundry was using the same equipment to make the same products with the exact same processes, the soil at the foundry might no longer contain the same metals. The second problem was more serious: without probable cause, Smith would be unable to obtain a warrant in order to take a soil sample. Without a warrant, any evidence he collected would be thrown out of court. But Smith had the feeling that he could match the suspect to the crime scene—if he could get a sample of soil from the grounds of the foundry. If the analysis proved positive, he could come back with a warrant in the future. So, one night in late 1989, he jumped the fence at the foundry and scooped up some soil samples.

Smith sent the samples to Tony Fung in Vancouver and waited. Fung reported that he was unable to make any conclusions based on the samples Smith had provided and the 1977 crime scene exhibits. In particular, the soil sample taken from the footprint on Carolyn's jacket was too small to undertake a definitive analysis. "They told me it was 'of no investigative value at all,'" Smith said.

For the moment, Smith's hopes of a breakthrough based on the footprint soil were dashed. But by this time, officials at the Major Crimes Unit in Vancouver were following his efforts with great interest. And then he discovered a whole new realm of forensic science and realized that it could be the game-changer he had been looking for.

Canada Enters the DNA Age

I T WAS DURING a visit to the dentist, shortly after he'd joined the GIS in Port Alberni, that Dan Smith experienced a revelation—one that he first shared with documentary filmmaker Jerry Thompson for his *Witness* episode, "The Gene Squad," of 1989.

Smith picked up a copy of *Equinox* magazine in the dentist's waiting room. "And in this magazine there was an article about deoxyribonucleic acid," or DNA. Smith was reasonably well versed in the basics of genetics and how inherited characteristics are passed down through the generations. What he discovered in the article was that at the University of Leicester in England, scientists had learned how to interpret selected portions of a cell's DNA structure to create a genetic "fingerprint" of an individual organism. This DNA fingerprint could be used in any number of applications, Smith learned. By comparing DNA profiles of different individuals, it would be possible to determine if they were genetically related. Those snippets of deoxyribonucleic acid at key locations (called loci) on the DNA helix were the biochemical equivalent of the lines and arrows and boxes on a family tree. And then the author focussed on the forensic applications of the new science. Smith took particular note: "The article discussed ... how DNA had been used, on one occasion, to solve two murders in England."

On January 22, 1989, an English court had convicted twenty-seven-year-old bakery worker Colin Pitchfork on two counts of murder in the deaths of two fifteen-year-old women, Lynda Mann and Dawn Ashworth. His arrest came as the result of a massive DNA manhunt in which police took blood and saliva samples from nearly five thousand men and compared their DNA profiles with that of the killer. The Pitchfork case later became the basis of a bestselling book by American crime writer Joseph Wambaugh, titled *The Blooding*, and first published on February 1, 1989.

While the *Equinox* article had just scratched the surface of the investigation, it was enough to convince Smith that DNA could help solve the Carolyn Lee murder. One of the major sources in the article was Dr. James (Rex) Ferris, then regarded as one of the world's top experts in the DNA field. He was also based in Canada.

Smith decided to take a bold step. "I located Dr. Ferris. No one had told me I couldn't reach out for whatever I needed. I figured, I'm assigned a murder, I'm going to get on it," Smith said. Smith apprised Ferris on the details of the Lee investigation since 1977 and told him the physical evidence that was available—specifically, the semen samples that had been taken from the victim.

That the samples had been retained was extremely fortunate. In 1977, forensic pathologists extracted semen samples from crime victims to determine if the donor was a "secretor." A certain percentage of men produce a telltale substance in their semen and saliva that allows a serologist to determine their blood type. While it is not as effective as a fingerprint in establishing the identity of a suspect, linking the blood type of the suspect to the crime scene could prove to be one incremental step in bringing that suspect to prosecution.

Conversely, and perhaps more realistically with this test, the RCMP's serology section could quickly exclude a large segment of the male population from the suspect pool. The downside was that twenty percent of men are not secretors, making it impossible to determine even the blood type of the non-secretors from a cast-off semen sample. The man who raped Carolyn Lee was not a secretor, and so, according to the science available in 1977, the semen sample was worthless.

In most cases, these unusable samples would have been tossed out as the case grew cold and colder. It was an indication of how determined Port Alberni investigators were to find Carolyn's killer that this presumably worthless bit of genetic material was preserved along with the grim photographs and soil samples and articles of stained clothing collected at the crime scene. Smith said Ferris did not hold out much hope that the Lee samples would be of much use with the new technology that the RCMP was just installing at their main forensic lab in Ottawa. "Because of the way the samples were stored—not frozen or air-dried—they were likely degraded and not suitable for analysis by what was known as RFLP technology," he said.

PRESERVED DNA

Through his initial inquiries, Smith had begun absorbing a technical education in DNA and forensic DNA technology. What he had learned is that DNA is the chemically expressed blueprint of life on Earth. All living cells contain strings of coded information known as chromosomes, on which all physical characteristics for an organism are stored.

The DNA molecule is shaped like a spiral staircase. Each rung in that staircase is formed by a matching pair of chemicals: adenine-thymine (A-T) and guanine-cytosine (G-C). The order in which the rungs are arranged determines inherited characteristics factors like height and eye colour. The DNA code stored inside one human cell consists of approximately three billion chemical pairs of A-T and G-C. If the chromosomes on that spiral staircase were mechanically uncoiled and laid end to end, they would stretch to a length of about two metres.

But the amount of variation within the DNA structure is extremely limited, and ninety-nine percent of human DNA is identical. It is by studying the known points—the loci—where wide variations occur (known as polymorphic areas) that investigators can establish the identity of an individual human being.

The Restriction Fragment Length Polymorphism (RFLP) technique of DNA typing was first applied in forensic analysis in 1985 by a genetics professor named Alec Jeffreys at the University of Leicester, in England. At the time, the UK government ran the Forensic Science

Services lab (FSS), where the new technology was developed and installed. FSS had first employed the genetic fingerprinting system in 1984 to determine paternity in several immigration cases.

The RFLP technique uses a "restriction" enzyme like a pair of molecular scissors to snip out sections of the DNA chain from individual chromosomes. Radioactive probes are then attached to areas of interest on the membrane. These probes are used to expose an image on X-ray film, producing an autoradiograph, or autorad for short.

In RFLP analysis, the DNA molecule must be in its native double-strand form. The restriction enzyme cannot work on a single-stranded molecule. The DNA fragments are size-separated in a gel-like medium under constant application of a high voltage. Under such conditions, smaller pieces of DNA fragments will move faster than larger-sized fragments. After a predetermined run time, the DNA inside the gel medium is "lifted" or transferred to a sturdier matrix or membrane made up of nitrocellulose or nylon in a process called the Southern transfer method (named after its inventor, E.M. Southern). Consequently, the DNA fragments are permanently bound to the membrane by high temperature.

By 1988, at the time Smith approached Ferris, the RCMP was in the process of installing a modified version of the RFLP system in Ottawa. But now, after having his hopes raised, Smith had been told that the RCMP technology wouldn't be capable of obtaining a DNA profile from the degraded samples collected from the crime scene in 1977.

FERRIS EXPLAINED TO Smith that "there was a new technology coming down the pipe ... that could obtain a DNA profile from a degraded sample like the one we had." The new process was called Polymerase Chain Reaction (PCR), and it would prove to be much more effective for processing old or degraded genetic samples. The PCR process was developed by Dr. Kary Mullis in California almost concurrently with RFLP at Leicester, but the forensic potential of the new process was not immediately recognized. (Mullis won the Nobel Prize in

Chemistry for this in 1993, at a time when the new process began to be introduced into forensic labs around the world.)

Simply put, while RFLP cuts out DNA components from a sample cell, PCR makes duplicates—unlimited quantities, in fact. The "chain reaction" describes the replication process, using different enzymes, that allows scientists to make millions of copies of the targeted genes. Unlike the RFLP process, in PCR analysis, the gel screening stage to determine the viability of the DNA is not required. PCR uses repeated cycles of heating, cooling, and warming to replicate specific sequences of the DNA molecule. In essence, the PCR procedure doubles the amount of product formed in each cycle, i.e., from two through four, eight, sixteen, thirty-two, and so on, *ad infinitum*. A fluorescent tag allows easy detection and quantitation of the product formed. Progressive stages break the DNA structure apart into smaller and smaller components that are tagged using the fluorescent tag and photographed using the same autoradiographic process as in RFLP. The "chain reaction" describes the replication process, using different enzymes, that allows scientists to make millions of copies of the targeted genes.

In 1988, the infant PCR process was just beginning to enable scientists to obtain genetic profiles from minuscule samples taken from blood, semen, or the epithelial cells found in saliva. It would be nearly a decade—and several evolutions of technology—before the RCMP made a full transition to the PCR process, but within a few years, a few private labs emerged in North America that employed the first generation of PCR technology.

While the RCMP had invested and trained personnel in the RFLP system, even as the new technology was first used in active casework, the molecular genetics section in Ottawa was already investigating PCR technology. Most critically, however, the RCMP elected to wait until the development of a more reliable PCR system than the one that had been used at commercial labs in the US to analyze the Dhillon crime scene samples, with relatively poor results.

By 1989, when *The Blooding* was released, the author, Joseph Wambaugh, had already established himself as a master storyteller in the field of police work, both in fiction and nonfiction. When his latest bestseller hit the bookshelves, millions of readers absorbed a crash course in high-tech forensic investigation in a story that ripped along like the best whodunit thriller.

That included Dan Smith and his RCMP colleagues. The Colin Pitchfork investigation was to prove highly instructive as they incorporated the new forensic technology into their investigative repertoire. The world's first DNA investigation had its origins in Narborough, Leicestershire, just a short distance from the University of Leicester, where, at the time of the first killing, Alec Jeffreys was still hard at work developing his RFLP process of DNA analysis.

On November 21, 1983, Lynda Mann was raped and strangled on a footpath in Narborough known as the Black Pad. Using the existing serology of the day to analyze the semen sample collected from the victim, investigators determined that the killer was "a Group A secretor, PGM 1+." That meant the killer's semen showed a phosphoglucomutase enzyme reaction of PGM one-plus, which was high. After the sample was subjected to antigen testing, it revealed that suspect was a secretor with Type A blood. Investigators were advised that this particular pairing of blood type and PGM rating was present in just ten percent of the male population. That is based on a formula of forty percent of the population having Type A blood, eighty percent of men being secretors, and thirty-five percent of those secretors having the PGM+1 rating.

Armed with this information, the Leicestershire Constabulary launched an almost unprecedented effort to locate Mann's killer, with 150 officers assigned to the case. But the leads soon petered out, the investigation team soon dwindled down to two members, and the case went quiet. But then, three years later, on July 31, 1986, Dawn Ashworth was beaten, raped, and strangled on a footpath in nearby Enderby, also in Leicestershire.

Investigators subsequently arrested a seventeen-year-old suspect, Richard Buckland. Buckland had brought himself to the attention of police as a result of his erratic behaviour after numerous witnesses told police he had revealed details of the Dawn Ashworth investigation that had not been released by police. Under interrogation, the unpleasant teen told police he had spoken to Dawn on the evening she disappeared, which later proved to be untrue. He also revealed that beginning at the age of fourteen, he had engaged in coercive sexual activity with a girl his own age. Later, he admitted that he had sexually molested a nine-year-old girl numerous times.

Under further questioning, Buckland admitted to killing Dawn Ashworth, but he adamantly denied any involvement in the death of Lynda Mann. Investigators subsequently located both girls and corroborated Buckland's admissions concerning his sexual behaviour. Confident that they had their man (or boy), they ignored the fact that Buckland did not share the Group A secretor, PGM 1+ profile that their serology section had identified from the crime scene evidence.

And here was where the accident of geography intervened. There is some disagreement about how Alec Jeffreys at the University of Leicester became involved in the case—whether he was approached by government-run FSS or whether he volunteered his services as a concerned citizen. In any event, Jeffreys subjected the crime scene evidence to DNA analysis, along with a blood sample taken from Buckland. By way of DNA profiling, Jeffreys was able to prove that indeed, both girls were raped and killed by the same man. But it wasn't Buckland.

THE PRIMARY LESSON of this case was that, just as in old-fashioned serology, DNA fingerprinting is actually better at eliminating suspects from suspicion than in locating them. And the fact that investigators were willing to overlook the failure of the suspect to match the initial serology profile served as a caution to ensure that any new tools in collecting evidence become an established part of every investigation.

With Buckland excluded, the Leicestershire Constabulary, working with FSS, then conducted the "blooding" that gave name to Wambaugh's book. Investigators collected genetic samples, either blood or saliva, from nearly every young adult male in the communities where the murders took place. It had been determined that, due to the high sperm count in the semen sample, the donor was likely to be younger than thirty-five. The team collected nearly five thousand samples in a process that took six months.

As a result of the DNA manhunt, Colin Pitchfork was arrested on September 19, 1987. But as Smith and a generation of forensic scientists discovered, Pitchfork was not located when his DNA profile set off the alarm bells; the baker's assistant was identified through old-fashioned police work. On August 1, 1987, while drinking in a Leicester pub, a co-worker of Pitchfork's, Ian Kelly, told colleagues from Hampshires Bakery that Pitchfork had talked him into providing a blood sample under his name. Kelly said Pitchfork explained that he had a previous conviction for indecent exposure and didn't want to have to deal with the police. The matter might have ended there, but a female colleague at the table reported Kelly's admission to police.

Pitchfork was subsequently sampled and positively identified as the killer. Six weeks later, he was charged. Just four months later, after admitting to both murders, he was sentenced to life imprisonment. (In 2016, Pitchfork was denied full parole but recommended for transfer to an open prison.)

Another lesson for Smith and a growing list of RCMP colleagues was that, for a DNA manhunt to be truly effective, investigators have to obtain a blood or saliva sample from the guilty suspect. While DNA could effectively link the suspect to the crime scene, having the killer's genetic fingerprint would in no way replace the need for effective police work on the ground. But Canada would not enact federal legislation compelling a suspect to submit a DNA sample until well into the next decade, so on the surface, any DNA sampling would have to be voluntary. Forensic DNA testing was an entirely new police procedure that would necessarily result in the creation of a novel culture within the law enforcement community.

There were serious ethical questions that had yet to be addressed. Most critically, how long would police be allowed to retain DNA information submitted by citizens on a voluntary basis? During the Pitchfork blooding in Leicester, thousands of men were profiled solely on the basis that they were young males living in the area where the crimes were committed. Would police be allowed to retain their genetic fingerprints against the possibility that they might commit future crimes?

This question alone had serious ramifications. How many men would consent to a future blood sampling if they knew they would be permanently recorded on police data banks? At the same time, futurists trumpeted how DNA could be used to solve any number of crimes, major and minor. Police officials looked forward to creating a shared DNA data bank network that could be accessed by police departments across the country and around the world.

The new technology gave law enforcement and, by extension, governments the capacity to record and store the genetic blueprint of any citizen, posing any number of ethical and legal questions. Over the next decade, each jurisdiction that employed forensic DNA would have to set the ground rules, forged though legislation and adjudicated in the courts of the land. Along the way, Smith and his RCMP colleagues would have to learn new rules of evidence in real time as the higher courts rendered their decisions. They would learn, for instance, the legal distinction between a voluntary DNA sample taken from an uninformed donor and a warranted sample.

BUT THAT WAS all in the future. After conferring with Ferris and reading any available material on the science of DNA, Dan Smith knew that police work was entering a whole new era. And he was part of it. "That was 1989, and we were right on the cutting edge of the new science," he said.

Smith was also dealing with a full slate of routine investigations assigned to the Port Alberni GIS. While the Carolyn Lee investigation filled a high-profile compartment in his investigative mind, it was very much a part-time pursuit as he and his colleagues tracked down the parade of everyday lawbreakers found in any small industrial city. So when Smith filed those C-237 forms at regular intervals, he was not just going through the motions. Smith's updates to E Division headquarters included his ongoing efforts to have the crime scene soil analyzed for metal content, along with his inquiries about incorporating DNA analysis into the investigation.

What Smith didn't know was that his routine reports were being copied to the E Division Serious Crimes Unit in Vancouver, where Corporal Wade Blizard began to take an interest in the Port Alberni cold case. As Smith became snowed under with current investigations, Blizard and his colleagues at E Division headquarters in Vancouver began to turn their attention to Carolyn Lee.

IN JULY 1989, the Port Alberni GIS got a new team leader, Sergeant Dale Djos, and the investigative bulldog stalking Gurmit Singh Dhillon grew another set of jaws.

Like Smith, Djos was born in rural Alberta, but unlike his associate, he did not grow up in a big city. The Djos family maintained a farm in the tiny (about 700 people) community of Sedgewick, but the future cop had no interest in following the family tradition, now in its third generation. "My brother is still there, running the farm. I'm the only one who ever left," he said. "I wanted to be a policeman, and that was that."

The thrills were few and far between in his first deployment. After graduating from the RCMP Depot in August 1969, Djos was posted to Vancouver, where he lived in Fairmont Barracks for six months, protecting a witness in a major heroin case. "There were four of us, just out of training. We spent eight hours a day sitting. For six months."

For a gung-ho rookie Mountie, that first deployment proved to be a snooze. But once he left Fairmont Barracks and headed out into the BC hinterland, Djos would be involved in a succession of high-profile investigations and arrests right up to the moment of his arrival in Port Alberni. There was plenty of excitement at the small rural detachment in Merritt, where he spent the next year and a half. "It was a seven-man detachment in an area that was mainly mining and ranching, with twelve [First Nations] reserves. We had five hotels and a Legion to police. We ran a lot of prisoners through our cells—about thirteen hundred a year. Those are very high numbers for a detachment that size."

From Merritt, Djos transferred to the rapidly growing city of Kelowna in the Okanagan region. When he arrived, he was the twenty-fourth member of the detachment. By the time he left in 1978, after seven years on the Major Crimes Unit, the detachment had expanded to over eighty members.

IT WAS WHILE investigating the 1976 murder of Winfield resident Shirley Ann Baker by Harvey Harold Andres that Dale Djos learned to push the boundaries when it came to gathering evidence. Andres, a member of the Grim Reapers motorcycle gang with a long criminal history, had crushed Baker's head with a large rock after sexually assaulting her while her two-year-old son watched. "When police found him, he said 'A man came in the night. Mommy screamed, and he went away.'"

The Kelowna forensic unit went over the entire crime scene, processing every shred of evidence available—except for a light bulb that the killer had unscrewed to darken the light over the door of the four-plex while committing the crime. According to conventional wisdom, a fingerprint deposited on the hot glass surface of a light bulb would burn off almost instantaneously. For that reason, the Kelowna Ident team hadn't bothered to dust it for fingerprints. They had a number of surfaces to process, and it was a particularly horrific crime scene.

But for the young investigator's sergeant, Bob O'Connor, that only intensified the need to search for every possible piece of evidence to catch the killer. And that meant throwing conventional wisdom out the window. First, he demanded that the Ident team dust the light bulb. "They checked it, and it had Harvey's fingerprint."

In the course of the attack, investigators also discovered that the suspect had cut the telephone cord with a knife. If investigators could match the cut marks on the copper wire of the telephone cord to one specific knife, it would double the chances of convicting the killer. O'Connor sent the phone cord to the RCMP crime lab for analysis of the cut marks on the telephone cord. A firearms and toolmarks specialist determined that the knife had been sharpened with a particular type of stone that left characteristic striations on the blade.

Djos and his Kelowna RCMP colleagues eventually took down Andres at gunpoint in the parking lot of a local grocery story, but he hadn't yet been identified as the suspect in the Baker killing. The arrest was based on allegations that he had planted eight sticks of dynamite in the car of a detective from Prince Albert, Saskatchewan. But at the time of his arrest, the biker was carrying a buck knife. When the fingerprint taken from the light bulb implicated Andres in the Baker homicide, O'Connor had Kelowna RCMP send the toolmarks specialist to the buck knife factory in Idaho to help with the analysis. Thus informed, the lab was able to match the striations on Andre's buck knife to the cut marks on Baker's telephone cord. On November 7, 1977, while Port Alberni investigators were still grappling with the Carolyn Lee investigation, Andres was convicted of first-degree murder and sentenced to life in prison. In part as the result of his role in the high-profile arrest, Djos was awarded the Silver Jubilee Award.

Andres, however, later managed to escape from the Kamloops Regional Centre while awaiting trial on the Baker homicide, but he was recaptured. Following his sentencing, Andres escaped twice from the maximum-security penitentiary in Edmonton, and both times he was recaptured. During a severe snowstorm on March 12, 1981, he hid in a dumpster and made his getaway in a garbage truck. He was returned to prison after shooting it out with Calgary police on April 19. One year later, almost to the day, on March 11, 1982, Andres slipped out of the same institution with four other inmates; on July 6, he was caught after taking four slugs from Saskatoon police.

It was long suspected that Andres was responsible for the rape and murder of seventeen-year-old Shirley Ann Johnston, on May 23,

1982, following his second escape from prison. According to investigators, Andres had barricaded her in a closet and set the house on fire. She died of asphyxiation. In an echo of the Carolyn Lee case, the Crown did not have enough credible evidence to bring Andres to trial until the introduction of forensic DNA and the reopening of unsolved homicides in the mid-1990s. The Port Alberni cold case, in effect, kick-started a series of RCMP re-investigations dating back decades, and prosecutors learned valuable new lessons each time one of these landmark cases played out in the courts. The murder of Shirley Ann Johnston by Harvey Harold Andres would become Canada's second cold case solved by using the latest in forensic DNA analysis.

Dale Djos was also involved in a high-profile domestic terrorism case. On May 25, 1986, four Canadian Sikh extremists attempted to assassinate India's Minister of State for Punjab, Malkiat Singh Sidhu, on a dirt road near Gold River on Vancouver Island. Based on wiretap evidence obtained by the Canadian Security Intelligence Service (CSIS), Dale Djos and his Campbell River colleagues subsequently arrested four suspects. They were convicted at trial in February 1987 and sentenced to twenty years in custody. It was Canada's first successful prosecution for domestic terrorism. Later that year, however, the conviction was overturned when it was ruled that the wiretap from CSIS had been based on affidavits from an unreliable witness. The error cost CSIS director Ted Finn his job, but the convictions were later upheld when Ottawa appealed.

The Crown appeal came in June 1990. By that time, Djos had been head of Port Alberni GIS for a full year. But Djos needed no reminder that major cases have a tendency to play out over a number of years and that the investigating officers may be long gone from the jurisdiction as a case proceeds through the courts.

WHEN DJOS ARRIVED in Port Alberni in 1989, he found out that one of his investigators had locked on to a long-unsolved killing of a twelve-year-old girl, and he wasn't about to let go. "Shortly after I arrived, we were going over some unsolved files. That's pretty standard: you see what outstanding major files there are, and you can't get any more major than the murder of a young child. So you go through the files, looking for new ideas, seeing what can be done."

When Djos discovered the steps that Smith had already undertaken, including incorporating DNA forensics into the long-stalled investigation, he realized that the quiet, self-effacing corporal had the skills and the determination to bring Carolyn's killer to justice no matter how long it took. What Smith and Djos did not fully realize was that the E Division Serious Crimes Unit had also locked on to the case.

Slow Progress in Boomtown

WHEN CAROLYN LEE was murdered in 1977, the city was at the apex of its economic boom. The foundry operated by the Dhillon family supported the rise of industry in Port Alberni, making metal castings for industrial equipment. But the city did not remain long at the top of the economic heap, and over the twenty years of the Lee investigation, the city continued to follow a path of dynamic transformation and had evolved into a much different town by the time of the next case in which DNA played a key role.

Ten years earlier, in 1967, the twin cities of Alberni and Port Alberni had merged. Contrary to popular belief, the merger was not driven by the massive destruction caused by the Good Friday tsunami of 1964. For residents in the City of Alberni, the merger was prompted more by the fear of becoming the poor cousins of their neighbours to the south, the City of Port Alberni. Alberni had a very limited business district and relied mostly on residential tax, while Port Alberni not only benefited from the taxes of the sawmill, but that sawmill employed a large portion of both populations.

In 1935, the forestry company Bloedel, Stewart & Welch Ltd. received a twenty-year fixed tax assessment from the City of Port Alberni to build and develop the Somass Division plant on the waterfront. Ten years later, in 1945, they approached the city for a similar agreement to build a pulp and paper mill. The pulp mill complex, known as Alpulp, was built on the historic site of a Tseshaht First

Nation village called Lupsi Cupsi. The tax break was to run through 1965, at which time the City of Port Alberni would then receive the full tax benefit from both operations. In 1951 Bloedel, Stewart & Welch merged with H.R. MacMillan to become the single entity known as MacMillan Bloedel.

The tsunami that surged through the upper Alberni Inlet on March 28, 1964, meanwhile, forced the two communities to pool resources, illustrating the value of a merger. On the night of March 27, a magnitude 9.2 megathrust earthquake caused massive destruction in Anchorage, Alaska. Fifteen people died as a direct result of earthquake damage, while another 106 died as the result of tsunamis that struck the coast from Alaska to California.

There were no deaths in Port Alberni, but it was close. Shortly after midnight, after the main shock wave passed Barkley Sound, a series of three massive waves surged northward up the narrow Alberni Inlet. When the initial warning was issued, the city manager of Alberni, Jim Sawyer, took up his post at the old city hall at the foot of Johnston Road. When the water suddenly began to rise for a second time, he hurriedly jumped in his car and drove to higher ground. He was standing on the pump island of a nearby gas station when the power suddenly went out and the five massive boilers at the nearby pulp mill began to shriek in an emergency shutdown.

Unable to contact the city work superintendent, Sawyer stood in the dark as the massive second surge of water swept away log booms, stacks of lumber, dozens of motor vehicles, and even houses. The damage was horrific, and the two rival cities had to cooperate to recover from the immediate damage. But as Sawyer explained, the amalgamation process actually flowed from that aggressive, long-term tax incentive program by the City of Port Alberni to attract major milling and processing operations onto the waterfront. By the time of the tsunami in 1964, that policy was about to bear fruit in a big way, and the merger process itself was already underway. Citizens on both sides soon voted to amalgamate, and the combined City of Port Alberni became official in 1967.

BY 1980, HOWEVER, after decades of prosperity, Port Alberni's economy was in serious trouble. In that year, unionized workers at MacMillan Bloedel had undertaken a protracted strike—and won. For years, old-time members of the union (International Woodworkers of America) spoke with pride about how they "beat the company." But it was a pyrrhic victory. Almost as soon as the new contract came into effect, the company began to downsize and shed jobs. The community had already undertaken a round of school closures across the Alberni Valley as families moved out and the school population shrank.

At the time of the Lee murder in 1977, MacMillan Bloedel's Somass Division was running flat out. The A Mill had three shifts of workers; B Mill ran three shifts; and the shingle mill had two shifts. Three planers and a remanufacturing plant all ran three shifts. But through the 1980s, the company made major changes to its waterfront operations, installing more efficient (and less labour-intensive) milling machinery and shutting down first the shingle mill and, subsequently, the plywood mill.

MacMillan Bloedel and other wood processors had begun to rethink how they would utilize their timber stock. The concept, known as linear programming, was the optimization of available log stock. Up until that point, the plywood plant consumed all of the available large fir stock. But as it turned out, those big clear-grain logs would get a higher return by being processed into lumber than by peeling them for plywood. The plywood mill shut down, and to this day, those big logs continue to travel by road to the town of Chemainus, about 117 kilometres east across Vancouver Island.

Facing what proved to be a temporary downturn in the world price of plywood, MacMillan Bloedel shut down its Alply operation in 1991. The sprawling plywood mill had opened in January 1942 to supply the Allied war effort and was fed with large old-growth Douglas fir logs called peelers. By the 1990s, the supply of high-quality peelers was declining, and the environmental movement, in concert with several Indigenous groups, had already begun targeting BC forest operations.

In 1993, MacMillan Bloedel also made a decision to close down the two kraft pulp lines at the Alpulp operation on the mouth of the Somass River, throwing yet another two hundred people out of work. On a positive note, however, closing the kraft operation at one stroke eliminated the characteristic omnipresent sulphur smell common to most pulp mill towns, and the effect on water quality in Alberni Inlet was almost immediate. For the people of this once-booming community, it was one more uneasy trade-off.

In the mid-1950s, MacMillan Bloedel had installed a weir at the outlet of nearby Sproat Lake, effectively raising the water level more than three metres. Along with the weir, the company installed a huge above-ground waterline to feed clean water to the massive boilers at the paper mill. At the same time, a dam was installed on the Stamp River just below Great Central Lake, about sixteen kilometres north of the city, to hold back water through the dry season. By means of controlled water releases, the company maintained the flow of fresh water into the Somass River Estuary through the summer to flush out the pulp mill effluent.

The Stamp River and Sproat River join to form the Somass River. An unintended but welcome side effect of raising the water levels in both lakes was that it created a large amount of new spawning habitat for sockeye salmon. By the 1990s, an entirely new recreational sockeye salmon fishery had established itself on Alberni Inlet. During the same time period, the Department of Fisheries and Oceans had built up a hatchery complex on Robertson Creek, which flows into Great Central Lake. The Robertson Creek Hatchery became the main source of Chinook salmon on Alberni Inlet, with a secondary focus on Coho salmon and steelhead trout.

All told, by the 1990s, the Somass River flowing into Port Alberni harbour had become BC's fourth-largest salmon-producing stream. But even as new technology scrubbed the air clean of soot and fly ash, and the water in the harbour went from hazy brown to clean enough to swim in, the visible environmental improvements were outweighed by the loss of well-paying union jobs. You could hang out your laundry without worrying about collecting a layer of airborne crud, but it was small comfort if you were out of work.

ONE SOOT-PRODUCING OPERATION not directly related to the forest industry was forced to move from the Lower Third Avenue area. By 1990, MacMillan Bloedel had informed Alberni Foundry owners, the Dhillon family, that they were cancelling the lease on their Third Avenue property adjacent to Somass Division.

At first, the owners were confident that they would be able to relocate the operation to a new city-owned industrial park on Tebo Road. The new development was located on the south side of Johnston Road, just blocks from Alberni Mall. That June, the city council approved the move. Central to the relocation was the terms of the air emission permit that had been issued in 1980. The discharge permit was limited to four hours per week. The maximum allowable discharge rate for particulates during that four-hour period was 14.175 grams per second, to a maximum of 19.5 kilograms per week, and according to the city engineer's report, the foundry had stayed within that limit since testing began in 1980. But after receiving approval by the city in June that year, the move was shot down by the provincial Ministry of the Environment, based on the projected level of emissions and because it was too close to a residential area.

Unable to find a suitable location within the City of Port Alberni, the Dhillon family located a site just beyond city limits in the Cherry Creek electoral area. In early 1992, the Alberni-Clayoquot Regional District approved the permits required to move the foundry

SERIOUS CRIMES UNIT JOINS THE TEAM

In 1991, when Dan Bond, a seasoned RCMP officer, arrived in the Serious Crimes Unit at RCMP headquarters in Vancouver, Wade Blizard was one of the corporals. The unit that Bond joined comprised four constables, four corporals, two sergeants and one inspector-in-charge. Blizard had by now made contact with Port Alberni's Dan Smith and Dale Djos after monitoring Smith's activity on the Carolyn Lee C-237 files. "At the time, the Serious Crimes Unit was evolving from a review and advisory role," Bond said. "It had become clear that we had to become more than that. We had to be able to provide support." The role of Serious Crimes was to provide assistance to detachments outside the Lower Mainland. Bond emphasized that Serious Crimes members went in to those small detachments to bolster local investigators, not to assume conduct of a case. They would assist with interviews and interrogations, coordinate case files, and write requests for warrants. And if any covert operations or surveillance were required, those outside members were not identifiable as local cops.

The Carolyn Lee case demonstrated the need for the RCMP to expand its capability for solving historic crimes. In 1991, Bond and Blizard made a road trip to Port Alberni to perform a file review and to map out a strategy for obtaining a search warrant and for subjecting the crime scene samples to DNA analysis. "My role was to do an exhibit flow chart so it could be presented in a court of law," Bond said. "Some exhibits only change hands between investigators one or two times. Some might change hands forty or fifty times—it all has to be documented."

WHEN THE NEW foundry site in Cherry Creek District was approved in 1992, Gurmit Dhillon was listed as a caretaker at the Second Avenue plant, living in a trailer on the property. He was in police custody on a sexual assault allegation when Corporal Dan Smith asked him for a sample of his blood. According to the Crown, an Indigenous woman named Jesse Jack told police that Dhillon had, in the course of assaulting her, threatened her by telling her he had killed Carolyn Lee. The case was later dismissed on the grounds that the victim was extremely intoxicated at the time of the incident and would be an unreliable witness. It was another frustrating episode for Port Alberni police, who believed Dhillon had developed a habit of selecting extremely vulnerable women for his assaults.

When Smith first approached Dhillon for the blood sample, Dhillon told the investigator that he would contact his lawyer and get back to him. After receiving no reply, Smith returned to make a second request, which was also ignored. Once Dhillon was released from custody, the Serious Crimes Unit deployed four members to Port Alberni to maintain surveillance on Dhillon prior to conducting a search of his trailer. It was critical to establish that Dhillon was the sole occupant of the trailer, otherwise any cast-off DNA evidence would be subject to challenge in court.

Maintaining surveillance on a trailer plunked down next to a working foundry in a high-traffic industrial area posed some challenges for the Vancouver team, but the crew monitored Dhillon's movements and work habits for several weeks while awaiting the warrant. Then, on March 6, 1992, Wade Blizard and Dan Bond came to Port Alberni armed with a search warrant. Dhillon was back home in the trailer, and the gate was locked when Smith, Djos, Blizard, and Bond arrived.

Ottawa had not yet enacted Bill C-104, which gave police the power to compel a DNA sample, and the Section 80 Charter prohibition on "unreasonable search and seizure" had yet to be thoroughly tested at the Supreme Court level. Even "search," now defined as "an intrusion by an agent of the state into a person's reasonable expectation of privacy," had yet to be codified in practice. Nearly fifteen years had passed since Carolyn Lee's murder. There was no expectation that the investigators would find any physical evidence, such as a weapon or a pair of boots with a characteristic footprint, linking Dhillon to the crime scene. What they were looking for, in the absence of Dhillon's consent to submit a blood sample, was anything that could provide cast-off DNA, such as a cigarette butt in an ashtray, a bloodstained Band-Aid in a wastebasket, or a semen-stained bedsheet—even flakes of dandruff on a hairbrush.

Knowing he was wading into untested waters, Smith had decided to limit his risks if possible. To start with, he had to climb over the gate to get to Dhillon's front door, search warrant in hand. "Mr. Dhillon came to the door and asked what this was all about. I explained that I had previously asked his consent for a sample of blood for DNA, and he had not consented, so I had gotten a search warrant to search his house for that material."

Smith didn't know if Dhillon had sought legal advice. Smith was fully prepared to take the team into the trailer and gather potential cast-off DNA. But Dhillon then threw him a curveball, and it later raised the question of whether his legal counsel was already anticipating an "uninformed consent" defence. "He said, 'I didn't think it was that big of a deal. No problem. I'll give you my blood for a DNA sample.'"

Knowing he was on uncertain legal ground, Smith made the decision to accept Dhillon's consent. He did not serve the search warrant and the team escorted the suspect to West Coast General Hospital. "We took him to the hospital, and Dr. Clifford took three vials of blood for analysis." In hindsight, says Smith, "I should have executed the warrant because the trial judge later ruled that I had used the warrant to force him to comply with a consent sample."

At the time, though, Smith had to grapple with the question of whether it would be considered "unreasonable" to search the suspect's house and go through his most personal and private belongings after the suspect had offered to provide what the investigators were seeking. "You execute the warrant and hope to find biological samples —and that's not a sure thing. If I turned him down, could he later say that was unreasonable search and seizure because I invaded his home to get something he's offering to give me?"

Dhillon's readiness to be sampled also raised the possibility that the accused had something in the trailer he really did not want investigators to find and that he considered volunteering a blood sample as less of a risk than a police search of the premises. Had Smith risked a ruling of "unreasonable search and seizure" by serving the warrant and collecting cast-off DNA, he might have obtained an admissible secondary source of genetic material in reserve. Conversely, he might have had both sources blown out of court.

The blood samples and the vaginal swabs from the Lee crime scene were first sent to the biology section of the RCMP's central forensic laboratory in Ottawa. Using RFLP technology, the reporting officer, Anne-Elizabeth Charland, performed the initial testing and determined that the results were inconclusive. With no usable results,

Blizard searched for a lab that used PCR analysis. The samples were subsequently sent to a private lab in Seattle, Washington, owned by Genelex Corporation. Thomas Wahl performed the testing, and in September 1993, he advised the team that he had identified one locus.

In accepted legal terms, a DNA match is described in terms of how many chances are possible that a particular person other than the accused would leave genetic material matching the sample in question. Wahl's findings disappointed the investigators. He said the odds that someone other than Dhillon would match the 1977 semen sample were one in thirty-three. "Not one in thirty-three trillion—one in thirty-three," Smith said. "There was a match, but because of the primitive nature of the technology of the time, the odds were one in thirty-three."

A year later, Blizard sent a sample to another PCR lab in the US, Roche Biomedical Laboratories in North Carolina. This time, analyst Richard Guerrieri produced a five-loci profile that improved the odds to one in thirty-four hundred. It wasn't enough to take to court, but by compounding the odds that were indicated at different loci in subsequent tests, it would later prove possible to establish the sort of probabilities that the Crown would need to bring the case to court.

A WITNESS COMES FORWARD

While the case against Gurmit Dhillon had evolved into a full-fledged technical marathon involving an entire team of forensic specialists and investigators, it was an ordinary street cop who effectively turned the tide.

By the summer of 1994, the crime scene samples and Dhillon's consent sample continued to pass through a succession of laboratories as investigators sought to achieve that one-in-millions match. Seventeen years after the fact, the evidence against Dhillon in the murder of Carolyn Lee amounted to a set of tire tracks, two acquittals on unrelated sexual assault charges, and the recollections of an ex-wife, recorded six years after the crime. While the DNA match was gradually confirming Dhillon as one contributor to those degraded crime scene samples, that factor, in and of itself, could not be included in the equation. What the investigators needed was one solid piece of evidence, such as a witness who could connect the suspect to the crime. Then it happened.

Constable Bruce Nicholson arrived in Port Alberni in January of 1987, just two years after beginning his RCMP training at the Depot in Regina, Saskatchewan. Nicholson and a classmate, Constable Craig Andrychuk, set up in a rented house in Cameron Heights, overlooking the harbour. There, the single young Mounties met Janet Lazorko, who lived just a few doors away with her mother, Alice. Nicholson and Andrychuk struck up a social relationship with Janet Lazorko, who was in her early twenties. "We became very good friends," Nicholson recalled. "Periodically, they would invite me over for dinner—taking pity on the poor single guy. Through the years after that, Janet and I stayed friends, and whenever Alice saw me, she would call me 'son.'"

In July of 1994, while biologist Richard Guerrieri was completing his DNA report at Roche Biomedical Labs in North Carolina, Alice Lazorko made the decision to break her silence on what she had seen on the day of the Carolyn Lee disappearance. There was only one person in authority she could bring herself to trust.

"I hadn't heard from the Lazorkos for a few years," Nicholson recalled, "and I was at work when I got a call from Alice." At first, his former neighbour sounded very reluctant to say what was on her mind and why she had called him at work. "She was very aloof, saying she had something that was really bothering her. I said, 'Alice, you can tell me anything. Tell me what's bothering you.'" There followed a long silence.

"She said, 'I'm scared, Nick. I'm scared.' I asked her if she had done something wrong. She said, 'I haven't done anything wrong, but I'm scared to talk to you about this.'"

Nicholson instinctively knew this was something she wasn't able to talk about over the phone. The two made plans to sit down, face to face. Alice arrived, accompanied by her daughter, Janet. "As soon as she saw me, [Alice] broke down. She blubbered and bawled. I realized something serious was about to happen here."

"She asked me if I knew about the Carolyn Lee murder case," he said. "I told her I knew it was a cold case, but we weren't really privy to what they [the General Investigation Section] worked on." As Nicholson listened and took notes, Lazorko gave him a detailed and emotional account of a chance meeting between two vehicles at Third Avenue and Ship Creek Road on April 14, 1977. Twenty-two years later, Nicholson recounted her statement to me, sketching out the route on paper.

"She was leaving Cameron Heights, driving down Motion Drive and turning onto Third Avenue. She said there was a large SUV coming south on Third. She was by herself. Just as that vehicle turned onto Ship Creek, she passed it. I'm not sure if she told me it was baby blue.

"She said there was an Indo-Canadian male driving, and as she got parallel to that vehicle, she saw a little Asian girl who appeared to be crying [Nicholson gestured, banging his fists as if against a window], up against the window as if she was screaming for help. She said she saw a blond man pull the little girl down in the SUV. The vehicle went up Ship Creek, and Lazorko continued on her way.

"The next day, she heard on the news that Carolyn Lee had gone missing. She told me, when she found that out, it ripped her guts out. She lived with that image in her head for many years, but she was too afraid to tell anybody. She lived with that for [seventeen] years."

But there continues to be a nagging discrepancy in Lazorko's version of the sighting on Third Avenue. At the trial, Lazorko said her first impression was that the girl in the car was fifteen or sixteen years old, and she couldn't figure out why a complete stranger was yelling at her. The image that registered was of a snarky sixteen-year-old instead of a terrified twelve-year-old. When, the next day, she heard that a twelve-year-old Chinese girl had been murdered near Cox Lake, she said she did not make the connection, and pushed the entire incident, uneasily, into the back of her mind.

But one day, many years later, Lazorko recalled the blond man and came to a sudden realization: his eyes had bulged when he'd looked at Lazorko because he'd thought she was a cop. When he realized that she was driving a decommissioned police car, he started to laugh.

Nicholson said that whatever recollection Alice Lazorko brought to court in December 1998, she had initially told him that, early on, she realized the girl was Carolyn Lee. "From my knowledge, she told me it was a younger girl," he said, noting that her visual estimate at the time was of a girl from nine to twelve years of age. "That's what she told me."

Nicholson said he immediately relayed this information to Dan Smith. At that point, he had no idea that Lazorko's description of both the driver and the vehicle matched that of long-time suspect Gurmit Dhillon. "I had heard rumours that Dan was in the forefront of 'the DNA tool' for police in Canada, but I still didn't know anything about it."

Nicholson told me he hadn't realized that Lazorko's statement to police would provide substantial grounds for the critical DNA warrant and for Dhillon's subsequent arrest. Looking back, he does not believe Lazorko intentionally withheld information, but rather that she was suffering from internal stresses, compounded by guilt after the fact, which prevented her from acknowledging what she had witnessed.

"My understanding was she sat on it all those years because she was fearful." Dan Smith agrees. He remembers her as "a very valuable witness. She came across as absolutely forthright and honest. There was no guile there at all. I have no doubt what she testified to was to the best of her recollection," he said. "She was very forthcoming. I got the impression that she felt guilty for not phoning sooner."

With Lazorko's witness statement at hand, Smith bumped the information up the ladder. "I took the statement from her and that became part of the investigational file. Dale [Djos] was made well aware of that as my supervisor. Ultimately, all of this got forwarded to Darrill Prevett," the regional Crown counsel who would become the go-to prosecutor for DNA cases in the province. The statement was earmarked as part of the overall objective of obtaining a DNA warrant.

THE LAZORKO STATEMENT was not a magic bullet, but it was one more link in the chain of evidence. Smith said, "I was certainly aware of the significance of it. But it wasn't in and of itself enough for a DNA warrant. It just formed part of the totality of the circumstances. There were also some things that I had to overcome—to explain in the DNA warrant." He explained that, when drafting a warrant, the investigator cannot simply cherry-pick the information that goes into the application. "You have to put in the bad with the good. You have to include things that would tend to exonerate the accused as well as to implicate him."

By the time of her statement, Lazorko had become aware that an Indo-Canadian male by the name of Gurmit Dhillon was the prime suspect. That potentially damaging fact had to be included in the warrant application. Dhillon had previously taken a polygraph test and, in the opinion of the polygrapher, passed it. A second polygraph, conducted in 1984, proved less conclusive. Based on that, he had been removed from suspicion and was no longer a viable suspect in the eyes of the investigation team of the day.

Nevertheless, Alice Lazorko's statement "formed part of our grounds for the DNA warrant," says Smith. "And the DNA evidence was the single most important piece of evidence in convicting Mr. Dhillon."

Alice Lazorko passed away on June 17, 2012.

The Law Catches Up with Science

IN THE SPRING of 1995, Bill C-104, commonly referred to as the DNA warrant law—which would compel a suspect to submit a sample of blood and/or saliva for DNA analysis—continued its journey through the Canadian Parliament. On June 22, the new legislation was passed in the House of Commons with the unanimous consent of all parties, including Nanaimo-Alberni MP Bill Gilmour and his Reform Party.

Following approval in the House, Bill C-104 was sent to the Senate, where it received Second Reading on June 27. The bill was then referred to the Senate Standing Committee on Legal and Constitutional Affairs, which held two public meetings. The Standing Committee sent the bill back to the Senate on July 11, with a recommendation that the minister of justice give adult offenders the right to have counsel present when a DNA sample was collected.

Bill C-104 received Royal Assent on July 13 and was proclaimed into law the same day. In August, Jane M. Allain of the Canadian Parliament's Law and Government Division prepared a paper, *Forensic DNA Testing: Legal Background to Bill C-104*, which, along with a short history of the legislation, spelled out in detail how the new law would operate and the offences for which it could be employed. Under the new law, a provincial court judge would be able to issue a warrant authorizing a police officer to obtain a blood or saliva sample for DNA analysis. The list of crimes under which a DNA sample could be compelled was extensive, including obvious Criminal Code crimes such as murder and sexual assault, but also encompassing offences against public safety such as piracy and hijacking or failure to stop at the scene of an accident. Property offences calling for a DNA warrant included robbery and break-and-enter with the intent to commit an indictable offence. Yet to be determined was the creation of a DNA data bank and the use of DNA profiles to investigate previously unsolved crimes.

With Bill C-104 now passed into law, the Carolyn Lee investigation team no longer had to rely on the legal admissibility of the voluntary DNA sample provided by Gurmit Dhillon on March 6, 1992.

In the fall of 1994, in *R. v. Borden*, the Supreme Court of Canada ruled that DNA obtained through a voluntary blood sample related to one investigation could not be applied to a second, unrelated crime. While *R. v. Borden* did not, on the surface, present any obstacle in the Dhillon investigation, it had thrown the entire issue of consent samples into a grey area. The challenge now, for Dan Smith, was to build a case to obtain a DNA warrant under the new law.

TRANSITION AT SERIOUS CRIMES

In 1995, Wade Blizard was promoted to sergeant and transferred to the Chilliwack detachment, and Dan Bond took over the case at the Serious Crimes Unit level in Vancouver. "I maintained a liaison with Dan [Smith] and Dale [Djos]," Bond said. "But Wade always kept his fingers in—we all just wanted to keep things moving."

Bond said while he worked seventeen homicides during his four years in Serious Crimes, the Carolyn Lee case had a way of hooking an investigator in. "Any police officer who had ever taken a hand in it—the only thing they wanted was justice for Carolyn," he said. "There were glimmers of hope with the DNA; there were stages when real progress was made, then things would slow down. It was a case of making incremental advances."

As an investigator, he knew that this was history in the making. "Everybody knew we were on the precipice," Bond said. "This was an emerging new field of criminal law—and we were part of it." However, Bond explained, Serious Crimes still placed a priority on active cases. Historic cases, while they were compelling, had to take a back seat. Still, there was general agreement that cases like the Carolyn Lee one must be moved forward as time and resources allowed. "When our phone wasn't ringing off the hook, we would undertake a file review. We would have to do that off the side of our desks."

Bond said that the RCMP recognized the need to increase resources to investigate historic crimes. The unit would expand significantly over the next decade, but at this time, it was limited to twelve members. Then, in July 1995, Bond was assigned to the Air India investigation, although he still worked out of the Vancouver office.

Bond followed the Lee case as it proceeded to court ("I did devote a lot of my career to that investigation," he noted), but by that time, Serious Crimes had moved to the Surrey-Newton detachment.

STREET KILLING

As 1996 dawned, Dan Smith and the extended investigation team continued to build up their case for a DNA warrant on Gurmit Dhillon in order to acquire that legally bulletproof genetic fingerprint they needed. Then, in the early morning hours of January 11, a seventy-year-old retired army officer was murdered in Port Alberni in an attack that was as shocking as it was utterly senseless. The case would add another strand to the future States case.

As the scene was later reconstructed, George Colonel Evenson ("Colonel" was Evenson's middle name, not his army rank) was walking on the sidewalk on Third Avenue near his home on Melrose Street when he was accosted by eighteen-year-old Thomas William (Tommy) George. Evenson was well known and well liked in the neighbourhood. It was his habit to rise early and walk a regular route, picking up cans and bottles. He donated the proceeds from his morning ritual to the nearby Bread of Life soup kitchen.

According to police, on the morning of the killing, Tommy George had moments earlier fled a nearby home in an agitated state. Defence counsel Adrian Brooks would later maintain that his client had been consuming hallucinogenic mushrooms just prior to the crime, rendering him incapable of forming criminal intent to commit murder. Investigators were unable to establish any previous contact between the agitated young man and the unsuspecting senior. For reasons never explained, George threw the elderly man to the sidewalk and smashed in his skull, striking him multiple blows with a large rock. He then rolled the body down a nearby embankment on the Coal Creek gully. Neighbours soon discovered Evenson's body, and George was apprehended the next day.

"We were on him," said Djos. "We knew he had been on the trail, and we got on him right away." But while a quick arrest meant they could dial back the hunt, the often slow, methodical process of building a case had just begun. "You shift into prosecution mode," Djos explained. "Evidence. Lab work. Autopsy reports. Do we have DNA evidence? All of these things have to be addressed. You have one chance to do the right thing, or you can lose the whole case." In short, the room temperature drops, but the sense of urgency remains.

Despite the early apprehension, the Tommy George case would spin out in the court system for the next six years, even as the investigation and prosecution into Port Alberni's second murder of a young girl maintained its own slow but inexorable course.

DNA WARRANT EXECUTED

On March 8, 1996, based in part on the new evidence from Alice Lazorko, Dan Smith obtained a court-ordered blood sample from Dhillon through a DNA warrant issued under the new federal law. The sample, along with the original 1977 crime scene samples, was sent to the RCMP's central forensic laboratory in Ottawa. By now, the Ottawa lab had made the transition to PCR analysis—although the Vancouver RCMP lab would continue to employ RFLP analysis well into the next year. This time, analyst Anne-Elizabeth Charland reported that the odds had now improved to one in thirty-eight thousand, based on a four-loci match on the 1977 samples.

Once more, the results had improved, but it still wasn't the sort of overwhelming odds that would convince a jury beyond a reasonable doubt. But by now, Smith was growing more comfortable with DNA theory, and he had become convinced that, because the Genelex, Roche Biomedical, and RCMP labs had matched different gene sequences at different loci, the odds would multiply exponentially. Smith made his case to prosecutor Darrill Prevett, who subsequently located Dr. Ranajit Chakraborty, an expert in human population genetics, statistics, and demography, from the Human Genetics Center of the School of Public Health at the University of Texas. Prevett phoned Chakraborty to see if Smith's theory was correct.

"The doctor said, 'The policeman is right. It's called the 'product rule'—assuming that all three DNA analyses are separate, that there is no overlap, and they are looking at different places on the DNA molecule, then you can indeed do the math.'" So Prevett sent all the data to Chakraborty in Texas. The scientist later reported that he determined that the aggregate of the three tests indicated a match of ten loci. Chakraborty estimated that the odds of such a match were between one in 151 million and one in 165 million for the Caucasian population, which includes people of Indian origin.

While the investigators and scientists considered the strength of their DNA cold case against Gurmit Dhillon, Port Alberni was about to be thrown into the spotlight for an active DNA manhunt.

Echoes of a Nightmare

F OR RESIDENTS IN the Alberni Valley, the morning of August 1, 1996, followed a heartbreakingly familiar pattern. A pre-teen girl had vanished from plain sight, this time during a public event. Early that morning, those living in the South Port area heard the whop-whop-whop of the RCMP helicopter from the Courtenay Subdivision as it made repeated low-level passes over the Dry Creek gully adjacent to the Recreation Park sports complex.

As a coroner with experience in homicide investigations and also mayor of Port Alberni, Gillian Trumper knew what that sound presaged. "I was at home when I heard the helicopters. I said to my husband, 'They must be looking for something.' Then I got the call."

In the parking lot outside the community arena, a search headquarters had already been set up, just blocks away from the *Alberni Valley Times* office. Reporter Karen Beck, whose eleven-year-old son, Gordon, knew the missing girl, attended the scene, and later accompanied members of the Alberni Valley Rescue Squad in one phase of the ground search in the gully.

The missing child was Jessica States. She was eleven years old and lived in the immediate neighbourhood. That week, the city was hosting a fast-pitch tournament at Recreation Park. Jessica, a talented multi-sport athlete, was a familiar figure around the ballpark. With her light brown hair cropped short and her choice of clothes, Jessica was often mistaken for a boy. Described as being "very energetic and lively," she was also possessed of a fiercely independent spirit, which her parents, Rob and Dianne, nurtured. As later revealed, both of those factors would play out tragically in the minutes leading up to her death.

Karen Beck reported that Jessica had last been seen during a game between Quality Foods and the Southwind Brewers, which ended just before 9:00 PM. When Jessica failed to come home by 9:15, Rob and Dianne States began a frantic search in the area surrounding the ballpark. By 11:15, they contacted the RCMP, and in an echo of that spring night of April 14, 1977, police and volunteers launched a hasty search effort that ramped up progressively as word spread and pagers went off across the Alberni Valley.

Complicating the picture was the fact that Jessica's blue Super Cycle mountain bike was nowhere to be seen. Given her independent streak, searchers believed it was entirely possible she may have ridden away from the scene the previous evening, only to get into trouble elsewhere.

CONSTABLE SHELLEY ARNFIELD was on the day watch on August 1. Arnfield had arrived in Port Alberni in May 1991 with her partner, RCMP dog handler Bruce McLellan. When the police chief looked at the five-foot-six Mountie with obvious scepticism, Arnfield knew she was going to have to prove that a female police officer could handle herself on the streets of a tough mill town.

It didn't take long. With five years of schooling in the same Prince George school of street policing as Dan Smith, Arnfield had already proven she could handle herself in a tight situation. With the endorsement of both Dan Smith and Dale Djos, she would eventually earn a slot in the GIS. "At first, I thought I would have to go in and break up a barroom brawl singlehanded in order to be taken seriously. But it didn't happen. I just had to do my job.

"I had only been on the section two weeks when I found out I was pregnant. So I went to Dan [Smith] and Dale [Djos] and said I was expecting. I thought they'd say, 'See ya!' But they said, 'Congratulations. Lovely.' They said if I was willing to do it, they had no problem with it." Smith and Djos also cautioned her not to get into any potentially dangerous situations. "Of course, you never know when that is going to happen," she added. For the next six months, Arnfield did stakeouts, surveillance, and, most effectively, tailed suspects. "Send the pregnant lady out," she recalls them saying. "Nobody's going to think she's a cop." She proved to be a valuable asset to the team.

"I came in at seven in the morning [on the day after Jessica's disappearance], and we've got a missing child. I got assigned to go with the helicopters. We flew around for hours, looking for the bicycle." It was slim chance, but it was one of the few options available for a wide air search. But the terrain wasn't promising, since the starting point at the ball field was on the edge of dense bush. Arnfield said the searchers were not using any high-tech tools like Forward Looking Infrared (FLIR) to detect the presence of heat (such as emanates from a body).

The bicycle proved to be a red herring. At 11:30 that morning, the bike was located in a storage room at the park, where the groundskeeper had placed it the night before after finding it in the picnic area on the boulevard across the street from the ballpark. "When we came down for a bathroom break ... that's when we knew that her bike had been found," Arnfield said. "We didn't go back up."

Beck, the *Times* reporter, had spent part of that morning with Jessica's parents, Rob and Dianne States, who by then were operating in a daze. "Will you put something in the paper for me? Something big enough that it can be seen?" Dianne tearfully asked Beck. And at that moment, she handed Beck the iconic school photograph that would haunt the pages of BC newspapers for the next five years.

The face that grinned back in the picture was quintessential tomboy, a T-shirt with just the eyes and ears of a cartoon wolf visible above the bottom of the frame. Had her life not ended so early and so tragically, one could almost envision, nearly twenty years later, Dianne States brandishing a faded photo to her grown daughter, affectionately noting, "You were a handful!"

Dry Creek Park was far from a foreboding place that parents told their children to stay out of. It was used as a living classroom for Port

Alberni schoolchildren, and walkers used it as a shortcut. The civic horseshoe-pitch grounds are located across a lane from the campground site. But this is no manicured city playground. In some spots, especially in the steepest stretch of the gully near Ninth Avenue, a few steps off the walking trail takes you into thick brush. That was the terrain that search and rescue volunteers had to contend with as the first day of the search wore on.

WHEN BECK DASHED back to her desk to write the day's lead story, her newsroom colleagues at the *Alberni Valley Times*, including me, maintained a presence at the search headquarters, cycling through until Beck could resume her lead role. She arrived back at the scene in time to join a shoulder-to-shoulder grid search down the ravine.

In the summer of 1996, the *Times* reporters processed and printed their own photos in a black-and-white darkroom. Each morning, one reporter would take on darkroom duty, developing negatives and printing photos for production. Darkroom duty also included loading the refillable film cassettes with bulk Kodak Tri-X Pan 400 film. One could load up to thirty-six frames for shooting sports with a motor drive or as few as a dozen for a quick shoot, but on average, the reloader put twenty-four turns on the hand crank with a few frames on either side for leader. But unless you reloaded and marked your own rolls, you could never be completely certain where your frame-counter was going to stop dead. And those final two or three frames were probably useless—exposed to room light during the reloading process. If you had flown back to the office on a hot deadline, churned out your top-of-page-one story, grabbed whatever rolls of film were sitting on the darkroom counter with leaders sticking out of them, and rushed back to the scene of the action, you were taking your chances.

Beck descended the hill with the searchers, snapping frames as she went. In these days of digital photography, it is sometimes hard to remember that right through to the end of the twentieth century, there was no instant replay on the camera, so when you found yourself in challenging light conditions, you shot lots of frames, bracketing your exposure times, and hoped that at least one shot would turn out. For a news photographer, it couldn't get much more challenging than shooting through dense brush in a steep gully, three hours past high noon on a midsummer day. Shortly before 2:00 PM, the frame advancer stopped dead on the last roll of film in Beck's camera bag. Frustrated, Beck rushed back up the hill to see if she could find another roll of film in her car or if another *Times* reporter was on station at the search headquarters. She had just reached the parking lot when she heard shouting from the searchers in the gully.

The area had been traversed by searchers many times already. But at this stage, Alberni Valley Rescue Squad members were conducting a slow, methodical, metre-by-metre probe of the bush adjacent to the trail. At about 2:05 PM, while climbing over a log, Rescue Squad member Stephen Adams noticed some strips of bark that had been freshly peeled from a nearby tree. Adams flipped one piece of bark off the pile and saw something pale and white underneath. The body of Jessica States had been deliberately buried under a mound of bark and forest debris. "If I hadn't moved the bark, I would have walked past it completely," Adams would later testify at trial.

Similar to the Carolyn Lee case, Jessica's body was discovered, relatively quickly, almost by chance. Dale Djos noted that, had Lyle Price not conducted a sweeping search of his farm, and had he not spotted the tire tracks that shouldn't have been there, Carolyn's body may have remained exposed to the elements (and scavenging animals) for months. Had Price not followed his instincts and avoided close contact with the crime scene, critical evidence may have been compromised. The discovery could well have fallen to a party of teens descending on the site for a summer drinking party.

In Jessica's case, the murder scene was just a short hike from both the ballpark and the campsite. Djos said it was fortunate that it was a trained search and rescue volunteer who first located the body. He acknowledged that deploying a civilian team in an active crime search does present hazards, especially when the suspect is still at large.

"When you go into it, the search is (hopefully) for a sick or injured person, even when you strongly suspect this is a homicide," he said. The Alberni Valley Rescue Squad was recognized as an effective unit with solid training, unlikely to trample over a potential crime scene. "You had confidence that, if they found something, they would ... stop immediately and report it. Which is exactly what they did."

Constable Arnfield recalled that while the discovery of the body was horrifying, it was not unexpected. "Everybody had a bad feeling. [RCMP dispatcher] Carol Corder took the call the night before, when the Stateses called her in as missing. And Carol has always said, 'I knew, as soon as I took that call, that ...'"

PARALLELS

Dale Djos assumed the role of lead investigator. Despite the number of high-profile investigations on his resumé, the sheer violence of the killing still haunts him. (And two decades later, the coroner, Gillian Trumper, is still visibly reluctant to discuss what she witnessed at the murder scene.)

As lead investigator, Djos was required to manage a growing team of investigators, to meet, comfort, and at the same time obtain evidence from distraught parents and family, and to act as the detachment spokesperson for a legion of local, regional, and, soon enough, national media. "Scene control is one of the most important [priorities], right off the bat," Djos said. "Having one person who documents every person coming and going at that scene. Otherwise, you can get all kinds of contamination." Even during the heat of an active investigation, chain of evidence is paramount. "Every item of physical evidence, when it moves, is documented. And a homicide investigation can produce hundreds of items of evidence. Each one must be accounted for at all stages of the investigation."

Constable Terry Horrocks was appointed scene manager. Horrocks visited the Dry Creek campsite and recorded every person who had been staying at the site, as well as the physical location of their tents or campers. Constable Todd Robertson was designated to identify all of the ballplayers from the tournament and to request that they provide DNA samples. The search also focussed on potential transients who may have been staying in the park.

The crime scene was just a few hundred metres from the *Alberni Valley Times* office, which was located between Third and Fourth Avenues on Napier Street. It didn't take long for local and outside media to make the connection to another horrific child slaying. "The parallels to the Carolyn Lee killing were obvious, especially to the investigators who were still putting the case together," Djos told reporters.

The reporter from the *Vancouver Province*, Greg Middleton, had once covered the ongoing Lee investigation as a reporter for the *Alberni Valley Times* and knew the territory well. Middleton was teamed with veteran reporter Barbara McLintock for this story. In their August 2 report, headlined "Girl's Murder Shocks Alberni," they cited a local ballplayer, Larry Hodgson, who said that, at about 7:00 PM, Jessica had asked if she could serve as batgirl for his team. When Hodgson told her the job was taken, she reverted to her standby role, retrieving foul balls for a dollar apiece. He was one of the last people to see her alive. "This is a big-town crime in a small town," Hodgson told the reporters. "We still haven't gotten over the last one."

On August 4, under the headline "Like a Replay of '77 Slaying," Middleton and McLintock expanded on the similarities with the Carolyn Lee case: "The murder of Jessica States is like a replay of the 1977 killing of Caroline [*sic*] Lee. The suspect in that 19-year-old killing lives a block from the victim of last week's tragedy." The RCMP E Division spokesman, Sergeant Peter Montague, advised that police did not consider Dhillon (who was not named) a suspect "at this time." The reporters noted that Carolyn had been abducted "a few blocks" (actually about ten) from the spot where Jessica's body had now been found. Middleton and McLintock gave a brief synopsis of the Lee case, referencing Sharon McLeod's statement to police six years after the crime. "The man apparently has a history of sexual assaults and a nasty temper," they wrote, and confirmed that the suspect had provided a DNA sample under the 1995 law.

UNLIKE THE KILLING of Carolyn Lee on an abandoned railway spur next to a potato farm, Jessica's murder took place in a very public place. Once again, members of the Alberni Valley Rescue Squad had pushed their boundaries by conducting a search for a crime victim with a suspect still at large. At the time Jessica was killed, there were hundreds of people, both local and from out of town, attending the fast-pitch tournament at Recreation Park.

In addition to the fast-pitch tournament, the annual Tlu-Piich Games, hosted by the Nuu-chah-nulth Nations, had also drawn hundreds of participants to Port Alberni. The Tlu-Piich Games included a range of sports held at venues across the region, and many of the participants were camping at the Dry Creek Campground, just metres away from the crime scene. Dale Djos would have to locate and interview virtually anyone who had been in close proximity to the park.

That level of human traffic at the ballpark and on the boulevard adjoining the gully where Jessica disappeared meant it would be virtually impossible to gather evidence beyond the immediate crime scene. The crime scene area was further compromised by the search operation. By the time Rescue Squad members discovered the body at 2:05 PM, the site had been criss-crossed continuously since 11:30 the previous evening.

The sheer level of violence inflicted on the young girl's battered body horrified everyone, and that included the professionals who dealt with homicide on a daily basis, Djos said. The initial examination of the scene suggested this was a spontaneous, frenzied assault on an opportune victim, with little or no attempt on the part of the perpetrator to cover his tracks, other than peeling tree bark and gathering forest debris to cover up the victim. Investigators suspected that a 375-millilitre Meaghers liqueur bottle found at the scene had been used in the assault.

A spontaneous, disorganized crime scene such as investigators discovered in the Dry Creek ravine frequently results in a quick arrest. Such horrific crimes are typically fuelled by substance abuse and are often committed in a drug- or alcohol-induced blackout. That level of intoxication and, in many instances, the loss of memory of the event, renders the suspect less capable of evading arrest—at least in the short term. Six months previously, Port Alberni investigators had picked up a highly intoxicated Tommy George less than twenty-four hours after the violent and senseless street killing of George Evenson. But investigators are always aware that the clock is ticking and that the first few hours are the most critical when it comes to breaking such a case.

"You've got to give it for the first forty-eight hours. Then the first seventy-two," Djos said. In this case, however, just as in the Lee case, investigators were dealing with an outdoor crime scene that had been subjected to the elements. The most promising piece of evidence, the liqueur bottle, did not yield any fingerprints. A remorseful, drug-addled suspect did not stumble onto their radar screen. Neighbours did not report seeing a bloodstained man fleeing the crime scene.

"We went door-to-door—every house in the neighbourhood," Arnfield said, "and everyone was coming out."

CRITICAL DNA EXPERTISE

When the initial, full-scale effort failed to yield a suspect, Djos knew it was time to shift to the long game. "After a while, there was a feeling it was going to be a campaign," he said. "It was my job to read every piece of paper that dealt with it. We often held three meetings a day. We were fortunate in that we had a top-notch steno, Diane Bonner." As the information flowed in—statements, briefing notes, voice recordings, etc.—Bonner typed up transcripts under the indexed TIPS format. The TIPS (not an acronym) information retrieval system is used in major files.

"You may have up to twenty-five different 'tips' with each murder. There is your autopsy report, neighbourhood inquiries ... There is the forensic report, lab reports, all your suspects, all your persons of interest. And it just goes on and on," Djos explained.

All of the information is cross-indexed. Bringing up one name brings up all references to that person. As the investigation progressed, it was obvious that the Port Alberni team of investigators was in for the long haul. The DNA samples were collected, the witness statements were collated, and the TIPS file grew exponentially. "At one time, we had twenty people working on that file because we had assistance from the [E] Division, from the Serious Crimes Unit," Djos said. "These are the specialists who work across the province, and they bring a lot of experience to bear."

Few police detachments were as well prepared for a long-term campaign as the Port Alberni RCMP. The team put DNA into the mix almost immediately. It had been eight years since Dan Smith experienced his revelation in the dentist's office, and four years since he, Djos, Blizard, and Bond had shown up on Gurmit Dhillon's doorstep with a search warrant.

While DNA had become an inherent part of RCMP investigations across Canada, Djos said that the police had not made it a priority to educate most rank-and-file members on the new technology or law. But Port Alberni was already on the forefront, and Dan Smith became a guiding figure at the investigative level, while Darrill Prevett, the prosecutor, took on the mantle of DNA specialist. Smith said investigators knew that the hard-won lessons learned in the Carolyn Lee case, with both the science and the case law, gave them a distinct edge in identifying and capturing the killer. While Gurmit Dhillon had yet to be charged, now that he had provided a warranted blood sample to back up the voluntary sample collected in 1992, it was purely a matter of time and paperwork before he would face justice. While the public remained sceptical about this new science, investigators were confident that Dhillon would be charged and prosecuted.

Faced with another child sex slaying, the Port Alberni GIS had by now built up a storehouse of expertise and had access to a network of the most elite forensic and investigative specialists in the RCMP. While DNA hardware was still evolving, genetic fingerprinting would be employed from the onset in the States case, and investigators would not have to work with degraded crime scene evidence.

"We all realized that DNA was going to play a huge role in solving this, as soon as we knew there was DNA," Smith said. "We now had plenty of experience. We were the first to get a DNA warrant on

Vancouver Island, and we were well ahead of the curve. We knew [DNA] was going to be a significant piece of evidence—undoubtedly the defining piece of evidence—that would help us solve this crime."

But there was still some initial uncertainty, due to the nature of the killing, as to whether forensic examiners could collect an uncontaminated genetic sample from the victim. As Smith described it, after "a few days of teeth-gnashing," the lab reported that they had isolated an uncorrupted sample that could provide a complete genetic fingerprint of the suspect. It was an appropriate metaphor.

The suspect's DNA had been collected from a discarded wad of chewing gum found at the crime scene. And so, a decade after the Leicester Police Constabulary launched their groundbreaking mass collection of genetic samples to catch a killer, Port Alberni RCMP initiated their own "blooding," incorporating all of the lessons used thus far.

By now, investigators worldwide had learned that DNA fingerprinting, like earlier serology analysis, was better at eliminating a suspect rather than apprehending one. But in a case where hundreds of males had been in close proximity to the crime scene, Smith said the blooding served as an adjunct to the interview process. "Because we had that, it was immensely helpful—and we took a lot of heat for this, I recall—in eliminating people from suspicion that we would have [otherwise] had to spend huge amounts of investigative resources on, unnecessarily."

And so the genetic manhunt began. Smith said those who could be positively alibied would not need to be tested. Those who couldn't would be asked to submit blood or saliva for DNA analysis. The ballplayers were the first to come forward. Smith said there were many motivations for men to cooperate with the investigation. Some felt the need to eliminate themselves from suspicion, while others wanted to set an example, to make a statement that anyone with nothing to hide should step up.

Constable Serge Cashulette was given the critical role of exhibit manager. With his excitable demeanour, coupled with frequent outbursts of profanity in his thick Québécois accent, one might question his ability to stay calm and focussed during the often-tedious process of collecting, recording, and filing evidence. But Cashulette was a thorough, meticulous exhibit manager who was especially popular among the community policing volunteer groups. One of Cashulette's favourite terms for street criminals was "shit-RAT" and this term became so ubiquitous that it was formalized under the Port Alberni police radio alphabet. It was not uncommon to hear very proper community policing volunteers casually referring to "Sierra Romeos" in the course of their activities.

Djos said Cashulette had to exercise considerable judgment in his role as exhibit manager. "Serge packaged up all the [DNA] samples in lots of twenty-four," Djos said. "He also had the responsibility for prioritizing samples [from suspects]. There weren't a lot of suspects coming out of the mix. I felt sorry for the guys at the lab. We kept inundating them with samples. I knew how busy they were. But they also knew this case."

IN THE LAB

A civilian RCMP forensic scientist, Hiron Poon, took over the case shortly after the blooding was launched. In 1975, Poon's family had moved from Hong Kong to Vancouver, where he completed his final two years of high school. Upon graduation, he attended the University of British Columbia, where he undertook a master's degree in pathology. In 1982, while he was still completing his master's, Poon was recruited by the RCMP. He went to work in the serology lab. While at the lab, he published a scientific paper that won an award and brought him to the attention of the powers that be. Partly on that basis, in 1987, the RCMP sent Poon back to the University of British Columbia to complete a PhD in molecular biology/biochemistry.

"They had decided at that time that we were going into DNA, so they needed somebody internally to train in the area. I was one of the guinea pigs who was sent back to school to learn the trade," Poon said. "Then I got recalled back to work in 1990, when the government 'had no money.' They cut all the training grants. So I went back to work in my old job as a serologist."

But in 1992, Poon received his first training in the RFLP process. Then, in 1995, he was selected to train in PCR. "I was one of two people at that time in Vancouver who were trained to do PCR ... When I took over the case," says Poon, "it was near the end of the RFLP time. We were switching over to a Multiplex PCR system."

The first analysis pointed up the shortcomings of the early technology, he explained. "RFLP needs DNA in really good quality. If the DNA is degraded when you run the process—this is electrophoresis—you end up getting a black smear, a streak, which is non-informative. That is the limitation of RFLP technology." That meant that the DNA could not definitively identify the donor—or the victim, for that matter.

Poon said that by 1996, the advantages of the PCR system were better understood: the analyst needed less material, and degraded material could be used to produce a profile. It was also faster— no more waiting for six months. "We made the decision that I was going to convert some of the samples into the new system. Then we got some results. We were able to derive the profile of the perpetrator ... That was the first break that we had: an unambiguous donor profile from the semen sample." Now, they had to find out who the DNA belonged to.

By 1996, public knowledge of forensic DNA was far greater than in the days of the Colin Pitchfork investigation, especially in Port Alberni, where the Carolyn Lee investigation was a topic of ongoing community discussion. There were those who were intrigued with the opportunity to be part of a high-tech forensic investigation in their own hometown. And there were also those who knew, thanks in large part to the widespread popularity of Joseph Wambaugh's book, that police would be extremely interested in anyone who made an effort to avoid being sampled.

Smith said the first to line up for DNA sampling at the RCMP detachment were those who were in no way under suspicion but who happened to be in the park the night of the killing. Later, the GIS would reach out beyond the immediate community to locate fast-pitch players and Tlu-Piich Games participants, many from the remote village of Ahousaht, who had gone home before being contacted by police. Again, the level of cooperation was far beyond what investigators had anticipated, and it extended to all levels of the community. "Even those who would normally not give us the time of day—like career criminals—would happily stick their finger out for a DNA sample so that they could distance themselves from this crime. There were exceptions, but the vast majority of people that we asked for DNA gave it."

One of the men who readily volunteered a DNA sample was Manjit Dhillon, the brother of Gurmit Dhillon, the Carolyn Lee suspect. By 1996, Manjit, nicknamed Munji, no longer worked at the family foundry, and his drinking was out of control. He was a familiar figure on the streets and at public events but not considered especially dangerous. Witnesses reported that he was seen leaving the ballpark in some haste on the night of the killing. But despite the DNA dilemma his brother was facing, Manjit Dhillon readily provided a blood sample and was subsequently eliminated as a suspect. "I could count on one hand the number of people that refused us. And I know that we got cast-off DNA from one person who did refuse us," Smith said.

With the DNA manhunt progressing, one individual on the to-do list broke from the herd, which immediately raised his profile as a suspect. "He lived in the area and moved away almost immediately after the murder. When we had approached him for a consent sample, he was quite agitated and belligerent. He accused us of trying to frame him," Smith said.

Poon said the suspect became a priority because of a genetic anomaly in the crime scene sample. "In the Multiplex system we used at the time, we found a number of alleles that we had not seen in the literature in North America. It was not in the database—not in the Caucasian population. When I looked at it, I thought, 'Oh—that is interesting.' I thought the suspect might have a black heritage." The suspect in question was believed to have that "black heritage." Early in the investigation, he moved to Steveston, on the Lower Mainland. "We had a surveillance team put on him. I went over and assisted, and in a short time, we had all kinds of DNA on him," Smith said.

The surveillance team at one point followed the subject into a bar and collected cigarette butts, beer glasses, and a napkin for saliva samples. Hoping they had spooked the killer into revealing himself, they sent the evidence to the Vancouver crime lab for analysis. Smith said that by now, police had learned the ground rules of DNA collection. This suspect had no grounds to claim unreasonable search and seizure. "By definition, there was no 'search,'" Smith explained. "He had no reasonable expectation of privacy for something he had abandoned. By now, the law was becoming more clear."

Subjected to RFLP analysis, however, the suspect was quickly eliminated from suspicion. Poon said the Steveston suspect temporarily sidetracked the States investigation, but after the early flurry of activity with one potential suspect, the campaign shifted over to the mass analysis of the volunteer samples.

"We had already started processing those hundreds of samples, but we could only do ten or twenty at a time. They had sent in close to four hundred samples," Poon said. He explained, under the existing RCMP protocol, samples were recorded in a system that skipped every other number. With nearly four hundred samples in hand, the numbers were now approaching eight hundred.

"While we were doing this, we re-did the samples in the Multiplex system. And then, two years later, in 1998, we introduced a newer system in PCR. So we did another conversion, this time to a unit that was available commercially. This was the Nineplex Profiler Plus system." Poon explained that the Multiplex was also considered a "Nineplex," but you had to do three separate batches to get nine loci. There was some variation in the specific loci tested by the various systems. Poon would later make the conclusive nine-loci (plus sex typing) DNA match with the suspect using that third generation of DNA technology.

In the beginning, the RCMP lab could only process twenty-four samples at a time, and the technicians were processing samples from all over BC. Smith and the Port Alberni team tried to make the best use of the available resources. "We definitely prioritized them with what were the most likely prospects," he said. By dodging police attempts to obtain a consent sample, the Steveston suspect had effectively guaranteed that his sample would be processed in the next available batch. Conversely, those solid citizens who stepped forward at the first opportunity slid well down on the priority list.

The job of the team leader is to tap into the various skill sets to generate results. "Dan [Smith] was continually updating himself on DNA law," Dale Djos said. "He's a very good investigator, the kind of guy you can put your trust in." And while the RCMP's paramilitary structure tends to place great importance on rank and bureaucratic procedure, the playing field is somewhat levelled out in a GIS room, especially during a major crime investigation. "It doesn't matter what rank you are, everybody is treated equally. You all throw ideas around."

To the chief investigator also falls the responsibility for managing expenses and reporting costs. In a hot crime investigation, it is customary to rack up a great deal of overtime. Much of that overtime (for regular members) was billed to the City of Port Alberni, but specialist members brought in from E Division, as per policy, were billed to the province. For Dale Djos, the goal was to justify expenses at both ends.

By the time Shelly Arnfield had joined the GIS in November 1996, the main blooding of the ballplayers and the Tlu-Piich Games participants had been wrapped up. Her job was to follow up on tips and to perform the odd DNA sampling as potential suspects were identified. As Arnfield recalled, a specialist came to the Port Alberni GIS and "gave us a course in taking a proper blood sample so that, when it comes to court, we can say that we've been trained in how to do it without contaminating it." It wasn't exactly a certification, but a physician delivered the training, and the GIS members were required to practice on each other.

MY EDUCATION IN forensic DNA analysis began around this time too. I had recently landed in the *Alberni Valley Times* newsroom. I had no journalism training, but I did have a master's degree in creative writing, and (more critically) I could run a black-and-white darkroom. After racing out and blundering into a potential bank shootout three weeks after I started in the newsroom, the detachment commander,

Chief Inspector Andy Murray, took me under his wing and provided me with a number of opportunities to learn about police work.

Over the next few months, I would be invited to test-fire the new Smith & Wesson 9-millimetre sidearms that were just coming into service, to join the local Crime Stoppers board of directors, and to receive a private two-hour session on the RCMP situational-shooting simulator, called FATS. And when Port Alberni was hit with a rash of pipe-bombings on Halloween night, Murray knew he could call me at home. When I advised Murray I was to spend a week in Vancouver working at the *Times'* parent office (Sterling News) in early December, he also arranged a tour of the RCMP forensic lab. By now, Murray knew I was familiar with forensic DNA and that I understood how critical it was to the Jessica States investigation. At the RCMP lab, I had a chance to learn about the latest forensic techniques from the men and women who made them work.

THE HIGHEST-PROFILE CASE

On Saturday, January 4, 1997, with members of the States family in attendance, Port Alberni RCMP held a news conference to provide an update on the investigation. Dale Djos told assembled media members that investigators had thus far collected 708 tips from as far away as Nova Scotia, opened 2,408 case files, and generated 3,445 computer files, but to date, had no firm suspects. Investigators had also collected 153 voluntary blood samples from men who had been in the vicinity at the time of the crime, and had collected 455 exhibits.

By now, Djos said, investigators were resigned to a long-term, highly technical pursuit. When asked if there was any significant, non-technical, non-genetic evidence that could establish identity, Djos replied that "he was not prepared to discuss that." When asked further, however, if, based on the evidence at the crime scene, investigators were inclined to suspect a predatory sexual psychopath as opposed to an impulse-killer triggered by drug and alcohol use, Djos was prepared to venture an opinion. "I would lean more toward the drug-and-alcohol-induced impulse killing," he said.

This was despite the fact that such a killing might be expected to generate a lot more physical evidence, he noted, especially when it was committed in a crowded area in near-daylight conditions. The Operations Support officer for the Port Alberni detachment, Corporal Lee Omilusik, interjected to observe that, in either case, it was quite amazing that, to date, not a single witness had reported seeing or hearing anything at the time of the crime. Omilusik, himself a youth softball coach, was asked if this indicated that the killer was very careful and methodical. "Either very careful or, as the States family has indicated, Jessica may have known the person," he said, adding, "Or he was very lucky."

Djos said it was entirely possible that that the suspect had committed previous violent crimes, possibly even murder. That raised the issue of a centralized genetic data bank for sexual offenders. "It would certainly be beneficial in cases like this. It is currently in the works, but it will be some time before it comes on line," Djos said, referring to the legislation that was proceeding through Parliament.

But under current laws, he explained, police could not simply go "fishing in the genetic data pool." Stored genetic information could at that point only be accessed by warrant on just cause. As contemplated at the time, genetic samples would only go into such a data bank if charges had been laid. Djos further noted that the E Division Serious Crimes Unit had commissioned a psychological profile to assist in identifying the suspect. As the officer in charge of the budget, Djos was asked how long the RCMP could continue to maintain a nine-member task force. As long as it takes, he said, adding, "This is, in my mind, the highest-profile case in the province."

A Double Landmark

O N FEBRUARY 13, 1997, a month after the States news conference, Tommy George, who had attended the same school as
the person soon to be arrested for the States murder—two
of the students the school principal had early on considered socio-
paths—pleaded guilty in a provincial court in Nanaimo to a reduced
charge of manslaughter. The Crown counsel from Port Alberni, Steve
Stirling, advised that he would seek dangerous offender status for
George when the case went to sentencing on May 8 in BC Supreme
Court before Madame Justice Downs.

JUST THREE WEEKS later, at 8:00 AM on March 14, 1997, exactly one
month short of twenty years since the murder of Carolyn Lee, Gurmit
Singh Dhillon was taken into custody to be charged with first-degree
murder. On that Friday morning, Inspector Andy Murray contacted
me at the *Alberni Valley Times* to announce the long-awaited arrest
and to advise that a major news conference had been scheduled for
that afternoon. Murray said the Lee family had been advised of the
arrest, noting that the past twenty years had been an emotional roller-
coaster ride for the bereaved family.

"It is important that the community understand that this is
a twenty-year-old case, and the RCMP has been working on it

continuously ever since the time her body was located," Murray said. "This was a team effort, from the work of the initial investigators through the efforts of the Port Alberni GIS, and the BC Integrated Homicide Unit." Murray then revealed that the Integrated Homicide Unit, already known widely as IHIT, had been involved since the previous year, when the unit began. He talked about how the DNA warrant law, or Bill C-104, introduced on July 13, 1995, empowered police to demand a blood or saliva sample for the purpose of DNA analysis. "It is a result of forensic evidence that we were able to make this charge today," Murray said. "DNA evidence was a critical factor in this case."

I asked Murray, for the record, whether the investigators had established any connection between the Carolyn Lee murder and the killing of Jessica States, just nine months earlier. "We have pursued that aspect," Murray advised, "and at this time Dhillon is not considered a suspect or a person of interest in the death of Jessica States."

Thanks to Murray's call to the *Times*, when the press conference began at 1:00 PM, my story was already on the street, released at the paper's normal early-afternoon time of publication. I had a twenty-four-hour head start on the big dailies—at least, the ones with a Saturday edition. In 1997, major media outlets still sent reporters and camera crews to press conferences in semi-distant communities, if the story was big enough. There was absolutely no doubt that cracking a twenty-year-old murder case with DNA was a big story. The TV outlets would file immediately, and the announcement of the landmark arrest would lead the news cycle. My follow-up story on the press conference would run on Monday.

At the press conference, RCMP media spokesman Sergeant Peter Montague broke the news. In his presentation, Montague noted that at the time of the Lee murder in 1977, RCMP investigators weren't aware of DNA as a forensic tool. He emphasized that, while the investigators of the day had no idea that the samples they'd collected at the crime scene would one day create a genetic profile to link a suspect to a crime, they had collected and preserved those samples to the best of their ability, using available technology. "That's why we place so much emphasis on crime scene evidence," Montague told the assembled media. What he didn't say was that it was probably a sheer stroke of luck that the genetic samples had been saved at all. According to the practices of the day, it was far more likely that crime scene swabs and smears, once analyzed, would have been disposed of as a matter of course.

Montague also revealed another significant landmark: Gurmit Singh Dhillon was the first suspect arrested as a result of an investigation by IHIT, which had only been set up the previous year to re-examine evidence from unsolved homicides using new forensic technology. Montague suggested that citizens could look forward to some significant arrests in the near future as investigators applied the new forensic science to historical cases. "There are three hundred unsolved homicides in BC, dating back to 1920," he noted.

Like Murray had done in our meeting earlier that day, Montague cited the 1995 DNA Warrant legislation that now empowered police to compel a genetic sample from a suspect. "We will now be able to solve many more crimes thanks to this legislation," Montague said, adding that this was the quickest law ever passed through Parliament. "There is no such thing as a statute of limitations on an indictable offence," he continued. "And if you can get DNA out of a fossil, you can get it out of a twenty-year-old [evidence] sample."

Montague stepped onto contentious ground when he declared that DNA profiling is virtually infallible. "This [technology] is not only promising, it's an absolute. [DNA analysis] is the most important innovation in the history of modern police work." That contention would come under fire when Dhillon went to trial nearly two years later. Montague advised that Parliament was still debating the creation of a DNA data bank, where genetic profiles of known offenders would be kept, to assist police in future investigations. That law would eventually receive Royal Assent five days after Dhillon was convicted. Montague also noted the switchover from RFLP to PCR technology at the E Division Lab. "As we speak, the lab is being expanded," he said. "We will be hiring more technicians and more scientists to increase our ability to process evidence."

Ed Watson, from CHEK TV, asked the same question Murray had answered earlier, a question no doubt on everyone's mind: was Dhillon a suspect in the murder of Jessica States? Montague stated for the record that he was not.

My follow-up story that ran on Monday, March 17, was headlined "DNA Legislation Cited as Break in Carolyn Lee Case." A sidebar featured an assemblage from over the years of front-page headlines in the *Times* related to the case, along with the now-familiar picture of Carolyn, arms linked with her sister Brenda. The sidebar recounted the disappearance of Carolyn Lee and the discovery of her body the next day, along with a recap of the advances in DNA technology and law. The story explained that Dhillon had been remanded in custody by consent and was to appear in Port Alberni Supreme Court on April 2. I wrote, "The matter is expected to be prosecuted by a team made up of local Crown Counsel David Kidd and Darrill Prevett. Mr. Prevett is the Provincial DNA Information Co-ordinator and is called in to prosecute cases in the province involving DNA evidence."

ENTER "THE DRAGON"

When Dhillon was arrested, his family retained Victoria lawyer Russ Chamberlain to represent him at trial. Chamberlain had established a reputation as a formidable defence lawyer, and he wasted no time setting the tone for the upcoming fight. Knowing what they were in for, the prosecution team wasn't about to be intimidated, according to Dale Djos. "[Chamberlain] came over to Port Alberni like a bull moose. He phoned [Constable] Shelley Arnfield and said he wanted access to all files. She said, 'Do you realize how many cabinets full of material there are?' Then we charged him by the page for every copy. He was pretty ripped about that. He figured he was going to come in and bulldoze his way around."

"We charged quite a bit for each copy," Dan Smith noted. "We were required to disclose evidence. We're not required to disclose it for free. There is a schedule of fees to be charged, and we sent that bill to Mr. Chamberlain."

This was Shelley Arnfield's only involvement in the Carolyn Lee case. There was a reason for that, she explained. "The reason I was elected to be there while he went through the file was because I knew nothing about it. So he couldn't pump me for info; he couldn't get me to say things out of school. I couldn't answer any questions." Arnfield said Chamberlain originally demanded "the file." By that time, there were boxes and drawers stuffed with the twenty-year paper trail.

"He was invited to come in and view it and to copy anything he wanted. So we wheeled a photocopier into the room, and he started going through the file. I think he was overwhelmed by how much stuff there was." Whenever Chamberlain found a relevant document, Arnfield would make one copy for him and one for the GIS, to keep track of what information he was using. "Not knowing any better, he wanted a copy of the timeline. I gave it to him, and I got shit later from Dan [Smith] and Dale [Djos]. They said, 'He's not entitled to that.' I thought, under 'full disclosure,' we had to give him everything."

This was one more lesson in Arnfield's education. While the raw materials contained in the files were fair game, the timeline as developed by the investigating officers over the years was considered "work product," and work product was considered off the table in the disclosure process. "I screwed up. But clearly, it didn't come back to bite us in the ass."

Smith said the disclosure process has evolved since 1997. "Work product is still off the table—you don't have to disclose it. But in my view, there's nothing wrong with disclosing it. Things that would be wrong to disclose would be privileged information. For example, legal opinions that we got from our lawyer or private information such as witnesses' addresses, and that kind of thing. Today, we wouldn't put the file into the room with the lawyer. He gets a disk with the file that we have vetted."

On Monday, April 21, Dhillon appeared for a bail hearing in Nanaimo Supreme Court. The suspect was released on his own recognizance on a $250,000 bond posted by two family members, who resorted to term deposits and sureties. Dhillon was ordered not to leave Vancouver Island without the permission of his parole officer, nor to apply for a passport. He was to live with his sister in Nanoose

Bay, to maintain steady employment, and to report to Port Alberni RCMP three times a week. Further restrictions included that he not be in the presence of any female under the age of eighteen, with the exception of his sister's niece. He was further ordered to abstain from all alcohol and drugs, and to submit to a Breathalyzer or urinalysis on the request of a peace officer.

CONSENT DNA SAMPLES IN QUESTION

The Liberal government of the time, led by Prime Minister Jean Chretien, attempted to pass a new law creating a DNA data bank to store the genetic fingerprints of those convicted of serious crimes. While Bill C-104 had given law enforcement a powerful new weapon, in the DNA warrant, to investigate serious crimes, the federal justice ministry intended to take the new technology further by creating a DNA data bank of convicted offenders. That stored information could be used to re-investigate previously unsolved cases or to link previously sampled offenders to new crimes.

Just prior to Dhillon's preliminary hearing, Liberal MLA Barry Penner (Chilliwack) took the unusual step of rising in the BC Legislature to call on the federal Liberal government to pass Bill C-94, the DNA Identification Act, before calling an election in the fall. "I'm urging the Justice Minister to take speedy action and bring forward the DNA Identification Act for debate," Penner told the House. "It will take time to get this program up and running, and we can't afford to wait."

Penner's plea was in response to Dhillon's arrest, which was the direct result of a DNA warrant. The *Alberni Valley Times* ran the story, with an update from DNA analyst Stefano Mazzega on the switchover from RFLP to PCR analysis at the E Division in Vancouver.

Mazzega had completed his Bachelor of Science in 1978. After graduation, he sent in an application to the RCMP as part of a series of query letters. "They [the RCMP] called me ... and in January 1980, I signed on as a civilian trainee in hair and fibre analysis, and I qualified a year after that." The new lab tech didn't have to wait long for a major case.

"One of the first cases I got involved on was Clifford Olson ... That was really jumping in with both feet." Between November 17, 1980, and July 30, 1981, Olson had abducted, raped, and murdered eleven children, both male and female, between the ages of eleven and eighteen years old. As the result of a controversial plea bargain deal, the killer's wife received a total of $100,000 in exchange for his confession. He died in prison in 2011.

Mazzega began training in DNA analysis in 1993. By then, the RCMP was using a slightly improved RFLP process. Prior to the advent of DNA analysis at the Vancouver lab in 1993, the facility had been divided into two units: Hair and Fibre, and Serology. When the new technology was introduced, the three disciplines combined to form a single unit. Mazzega noted that, by then, the RCMP already had DNA capacity in Ottawa and Edmonton, and the single-lab system had already been tried and proven.

In similar fashion, when improved PCR technology became available, it was first installed and tested in the Ottawa lab. The new technique was now well understood as being far superior to the original British process, especially for cold cases. "For RFLP, you needed a bloodstain the size of a dime to get a profile. And it would take you about six months to get a complete result," Mazzega explained. "The PCR was extremely sensitive, to the point where you could get a profile off a single hair root, if it still had some tissue attached. And you could turn it around in a week if you had to. So it was a huge step forward."

And as the law surrounding forensic DNA evolved, the new technology provided investigators with a more reliable method of obtaining evidence they could actually use in court. As Mazzega pointed out, RFLP analysis was great for those consent samples taken by a doctor or a certified technician. Typically, the donor provided that convenient dime-sized spot of blood and/or a generous swab of epithelial tissue from inside the cheek.

But the 1994 R. v. Borden case had thrown all of those consent samples into a grey area, making it imperative that the RCMP acquire the capacity to analyze cast-off samples from the most minute quantities of material—bloodstains, body fluids, skin particles, dandruff, dried saliva—the everyday shedding and oozing of daily life. Sometimes an undercover officer would provide a veritable smorgasbord of human sloughings from a potential suspect.

Mazzega told the *Times* that, until the new equipment was validated, the Vancouver lab would continue to use the older RFLP process. Until certified, any profile produced under the new technology would be subject to court challenge, he explained. For the moment, he said, the lab would likely add only four new technicians to handle evidence. That number would increase should the DNA data bank bill be passed in Ottawa as hoped.

"I'm still training on the new technology," Mazzega said. "We're still trying to provide the [DNA analysis] service, but some of our work is being sent out to other labs." The lab was expected to be fully validated and operational on the PCR technology by September 1997.

But Bill C-94 died on the Order Paper when the 35th Parliament was dissolved on April 27, 1997. In the meantime, the re-examination of crime scene evidence continued in the background.

ON APRIL 16, 1997, Arid Lacis, an electron microscopy specialist, received a number of previously examined pieces of evidence. Those included Exhibit 27 (the footprint on Carolyn's jacket), a soil sample taken from the murder scene, an earring taken from the victim (Exhibit 20), one from Sharon McLeod (Exhibit 37, found in Dhillon's truck), and one provided by the Lee family (Exhibit 40). Three months later, Lacis would receive further soil samples from the E Division Serious Crimes Unit. Lacis was subsequently unable to find any evidence from his examination of the earrings.

But he struck pay dirt in his examination of the grit from Carolyn's jacket. The analyst had been asked to examine it for the presence of carbonaceous particles, such as coke or coal, that one could expect to find on a foundry floor. Examination under a stereomicroscope revealed nineteen dark or black particles that were (possibly) the type he was looking for. Eighteen of these particles were irregularly shaped. One particle (tagged as Particle no. 8) was different than the others—it was a round bead. Further examination of the particles revealed a distinct difference between Particle no. 8 and the other eighteen particles. Particle no. 8 was an iron bead that originated from "a location where ferrous metals were cast, welded, or flame-cut." Like a foundry.

On May 7, Dhillon appeared in Port Alberni provincial court to set a date for a preliminary hearing. That hearing was set to last for five days, starting on January 16, 1998.

The next day, Tommy George appeared for sentencing on the Evenson killing, on the reduced charge of manslaughter. At the request of Crown counsel Steve Stirling, Madame Justice Downs imposed "dangerous offender" status. Under dangerous offender status, the convicted offender remains in custody indefinitely until the court rules he or she is no longer a threat to public safety. As it later turned out, George's "dangerous offender" status was quietly rescinded, and he would return to the community.

A PERSON OF INTEREST

On July 25, 1997, as the first anniversary of Jessica States's killing approached, investigators identified another person of interest. He had already attracted the attention of his former principal and a sequence of fellow students and educators.

Tom McEvay was the principal from 1987 through 1992 at the Port Alberni school then known as E.J. Dunn Junior Secondary School, where he first encountered an angry young man named Roderick Patten. For a professional educator, it is difficult to concede that some students are beyond reaching. Over his thirty-four years in the public school system, McEvay says he can count four individuals (including Tommy George) whose behaviour foreshadowed a violent future.

"You knew there was something wrong, other than they came from a rough background," he said. "These are the ones that—at the time nobody was going to say it—you wondered, are they socio-pathic? Are they psychotic? What are the issues they face? How they perceived the world and how they perceived other people was so different. Other people, to them, were just pieces of meat."

Roderick Patten had accepted an invitation to join the school wrestling team, and there were hopes he would benefit from the program despite the numerous red flags. "Roddy had many barriers working against him for success in the school system and also for coping with society," McEvay said. "[He was] tough and wiry, and I thought we had a really raw product on our hands, and, maybe, wrestling can be one of those salvations for this kid, where he is able to channel that aggression and toughness into something positive."

But in a program that placed a premium on mutual respect and social responsibility, this was a young man who made no pretense to fit in, and he eventually dropped off the team. "With Roddy, you could tell there were issues that went well beyond inappropriate behaviour. It went further than just seeing things in a different way. He really struggled with respecting others and taking responsibility for his own actions."

Over the years, Patten would show a range of different faces, depending on which situation he happened to be in. That was a pattern that developed in his early school years, according to Georgina Sutherland, who attended school with Patten, first at Eighth Avenue Elementary School, then at E.J. Dunn, where Tom McEvay was principal.

Sutherland said that being one of the few Indigenous children in her middle-class neighbourhood was difficult enough, and she was especially self-conscious that she didn't look like or dress as well as her non-Indigenous classmates. As she explained, when she first encountered Patten, she felt sorry for him. A bond gradually developed between the two children based on their mutual outsider status as Indigenous kids. She noted that while Patten's propensity for spontaneous violence didn't become apparent until junior high school, the tripwires were well established while he was still in elementary school. Eventually, she had to dissociate herself from the troublesome teen.

"I felt I already had my labels; I had felt discrimination. I was already poor and not well-dressed ... Native with short, ugly hair and stuff like that. I didn't want to get painted with that same paintbrush. I thought, if I didn't want to keep getting bullied like he was; I couldn't continue to stick up for him."

By junior high, Sutherland had developed into a talented multi-sport athlete. So while she continued to be self-conscious about her clothes and appearance, her athletic prowess gave her increasing status among her peers. Being associated with Roddy Patten had become a liability. "I didn't want to be the one who was getting picked on in the locker room for being the one that was sticking up for him."

For many years, the Alberni school district ran the Boys Project School, which provided alternative education for boys who were unable to function in the regular system. With a history of bullying and inexplicable incidences of violence that began while he still attended Eighth Avenue Elementary School, Patten was a natural candidate for the program, which taught basic trade skills in a flexible learning environment.

Jim Lawson taught at Boys Project when Patten was admitted to the program. Lawson taught Patten for one and a half years, and quickly realized that this was a young man who needed close supervision, especially after he was involved in several disturbing bullying incidents.

"He was the kind of guy who really relished that power of being able to dictate the emotions of another kid by using intimidation and physical force." Lawson described Patten's obvious ability to make other students fearful of him but noted that he also had "the charisma to get people to stand beside him or behind him while he went ahead and bullied somebody else. He had some pretty refined skills in doing that."

Lawson said staff members at Boys Project were generally spared the sort of violence and abusive behaviour that some of their students were capable of dishing out. And despite showing symptoms of disruptive and antisocial behaviour, it was obvious that even hard-core students like Patten felt connected to the program. "It didn't mean there weren't blow-ups. But as soon as that smoke blew over, they'd be back. I mean— we played roller hockey every morning. We had relationships with kids where they mattered to us. Roddy thrived in that environment."

An incident during one of those morning roller hockey games on the wooden floor at Glenwood Centre would play out years later when

Roddy Patten went to trial for murder. Lawson and Patten inadvertently collided and the younger player went down hard, striking the back of his head. "It was obvious that he'd had his bell rung, and he sat out the rest of the game. Of course, we didn't know as much about concussions in those days." Lawson said he was later amazed to discover that, years later, Patten's defence lawyer, Jim Heller, suggested at trial that the collision at Glenwood Centre had caused a significant brain injury that rendered his client not criminally responsible for his behaviour.

Looking back, Lawson said that, given the circumstances of Patten's childhood and the likelihood that he suffered from a serious personality disorder, it is unlikely that he ever had a chance to live a normal life. "At the time, I thought that he was a bully and a bit of a thug—and a kid who didn't have much of a conscience. If you can't ever make a breakthrough with a kid and have them realize a sense of empathy, then they are in serious trouble."

LOW-PRIORITY SUSPECT

But when Patten became a person of interest in the States case, he was just one of hundreds. "He was part of a circle of friends, all accusing each other of being the one who killed Jessica," Dan Smith said. When investigators attempted to obtain specific information from members of the group, they got nowhere. "It was like nailing Jell-O to a wall. Finally, we thought the best idea would be to get a DNA sample from the bunch of them to put the matter to rest once and for all."

When Smith initially asked Patten to provide a consent DNA sample, he balked, saying that he had to consult with his father (Patten was seventeen at the time). Finally, after several further approaches, he provided a sample, which went into the growing pool of blood and saliva samples at the RCMP lab in Vancouver. But as Hiron Poon, the DNA analyst, explained, with no particular red flags on his file, Patten's sample was given a low priority. "Patten was Sample 700-something," he explained. "His profile was about the second-to-last batch." He was, in Serge Cashulette's terminology, just another Sierra Romeo, and his DNA sample was taken purely on spec. Testing was still being done by hand, in batches of twenty-four, and the crime lab had plenty of active investigations requiring immediate action. As the Gurmit Dhillon trial approached, the Patten DNA was successively bumped down the line. It would be nearly two years before it set off the alarm bells at the RCMP crime lab.

Shelley Arnfield said that, as time dragged on, prioritizing suspects became more difficult. "When Serge transferred, I got placed as the exhibit person. At that point, we sent in samples twenty-four at a time. If you had a sample come in that was 'a stronger person of interest,' you might send it alone. But that only happened a couple of times. One night, I was looking at my exhibit book, and I had 152 blood samples left, and I thought, 'This is nuts!' Sending twenty-four off, waiting to get the results, packaging off the next twenty-four, sending them off ... I said, 'The lab can deal with them all.' I packaged them up—all 152 of them—and sent them in. Everything we had left, and that included Roddy's."

Despite the number of samples and the ponderous analysis process, Stefano Mazzega has suggested the two-year delay raises questions. Patten was considered low priority at the time the sample was taken. Most likely, he believes, the voluntary blood sample was repeatedly passed over until the switch to PCR analysis.

When PCR technology was certified at the Vancouver lab, the cumbersome RFLP system was eliminated almost immediately. Those samples that were still in play were routinely retested in PCR. That included profiles for both solved and unsolved cases, which were subsequently filed in the National DNA Data Bank. "The PCR technology arrived at our lab in 1998. [When Patten's sample arrived], we probably had our RFLP shut down, and we were rejigging for the new system," Mazzega said.

It wasn't about the crime scene sample, however. While PCR does provide better results from cast-off DNA, Mazzega said the RFLP technology available in 1996 was perfectly adequate to obtain a DNA sample from a discarded piece of chewing gum. Looking back, however, Hiron Poon said it was the vaginal sample that was critical in determining Patten as the perpetrator of the crime. Poon explained that the lab had both the semen sample and the chewing gum collected at the crime scene. The chewing gum would be expected to produce a better DNA result, but forensically speaking, all it meant was that the suspect had spit out a piece of gum near the scene of the crime.

The vaginal sample, however, linked the owners of that DNA directly to the crime. That being said, the vaginal material collected would contain DNA from both the victim and the perpetrator, as well as a plethora of biological materials, including bacteria, from both. Poon revealed that the description of the crime scene sample as "chewing gum" is deceptive. The type of chewing gum raised a number of strategic questions for investigators.

"The chewing gum results came in after the vaginal sample, and we found it was a mixture of two people, Jessica and Patten. But this was bubble gum. And I didn't think an adult would be chewing bubble gum. That made me think it could be [from] a juvenile. In retrospect, I think maybe we should have been looking at juveniles first."

How the bubble gum acquired two distinct DNA profiles is a matter of question. There are a number of possibilities, none of them pleasant. In one scenario, Jessica is chewing the gum at the time she is attacked. Somehow, perhaps in an act of dominance, Patten takes the gum from her mouth and chews it himself, then spits it out. More likely, Patten was chewing the gum when he delivered the "suck marks" later described in the autopsy report, and obtained genetic material from the victim. "Or he tried to kiss her," Poon suggested, with obvious distaste.

The large wad of gum was found under the victim's body at the crime scene. Poon said it is also possible that in the violence and terror of the moment, there was enough genetic material on Jessica's bare skin to transfer her DNA onto the gum. "That's what I think—her body DNA was transferred onto the gum. But definitely, his DNA was there."

While the integrity of Patten's DNA sample was relatively straightforward to prove, by the time Gurmit Dhillon went to trial, his defence team would challenge every aspect of the DNA evidence chain—even the validity of DNA science itself.

The Argyle Street landscape, from an extensive series of streetscapes taken in 1976, the year before Carolyn Lee was abducted from this area and murdered. Somass Hotel at left, Carmoor Building at right.
ALBERNI VALLEY MUSEUM

The Somass Hotel at the corner of Argyle Street and Kingsway in 1976. It was gutted by fire and demolished in 2014. ALBERNI VALLEY MUSEUM

In 2018, the Arrowview Hotel, with its checkered history, still loomed over the building that once housed the Pat Cummings School of Dance. Carolyn Lee attended her last dance class on April 14, 1977. SHAYNE MORROW

Looking north on First Avenue toward the MacMillan Bloedel Somass Division sawmill complex. In 1976, when this was taken, the sawmill had 1,100 full-time employees. ALBERNI VALLEY MUSEUM

Carolyn Lee and her sister Brenda pose for a family photo shortly before Carolyn disappeared.
ALBERNI VALLEY TIMES, COURTESY BLACK PRESS

The Pine Café in 1976, at Third and Mar, just blocks from the dance studio. Carolyn Lee was abducted on her way to the restaurant. The building is still there, now for sale.
ALBERNI VALLEY MUSEUM

Carolyn Lee crime scene. *ALBERNI VALLEY TIMES*, COURTESY BLACK PRESS

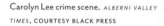

At the Lee crime scene, a pair of RCMP divers conduct a search for any object which might have been used as a murder weapon.
ALBERNI VALLEY TIMES, COURTESY BLACK PRESS

An RCMP tracking dog, brought in from Vancouver, at the Carolyn Lee crime scene.
ALBERNI VALLEY MUSEUM, COURTESY BLACK PRESS

On March 14, 1997, one month short of twenty years after Carolyn Lee disappeared, Inspector Andrew Murray, the Port Alberni RCMP detachment commander (right), announces the arrest of Gurmit Singh Dhillon on one count of first-degree murder. At left, RCMP media spokesman Sergeant Peter Montague. SHAYNE MORROW / *ALBERNI VALLEY TIMES*

This now-familiar photo of Jessica States, which the family gave to the *Alberni Valley Times* the morning after her disappearance, was first published while the search was still active. *ALBERNI VALLEY TIMES*, COURTESY BLACK PRESS

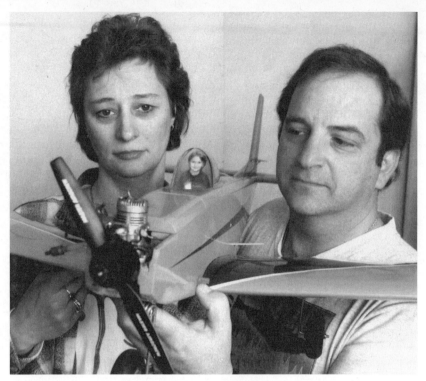

Dianne and Rob States with a remote-control aircraft "piloted" by daughter Jessica.
COLIN PRICE, COURTESY DALE DJOS

A softball among the flowers at a memorial set up immediately after Jessica's body was found across the street from Recreation Park. *ALBERNI VALLEY TIMES*, COURTESY BLACK PRESS

top For some time, the tree at the centre of the memorial was referred to as "Jessica's tree." *ALBERNI VALLEY TIMES*, COURTESY BLACK PRESS

middle Sergeant Dale Djos, head of the Port Alberni General Investigation Section, January 4, 1997, at a press conference about the States investigation. SHAYNE MORROW

bottom A weary Dan Smith updates the media on the States investigation at a January 4, 1997, press conference. SHAYNE MORROW

top Dianne and Rob States at the January 4, 1997, press conference to announce progress in the case. SHAYNE MORROW

middle Sgt. Dale Djos and Corporal Dan Smith at the permanent memorial erected for Jessica States, across the street from Recreation Park. COLIN PRICE, COURTESY DALE DJOS

bottom A stricken Rob States at the tree where a permanent memorial is now located. *ALBERNI VALLEY TIMES*, COURTESY BLACK PRESS

Landmark Trial Moves Forward

O N JANUARY 21, 1998, after five days of testimony, Provincial Court Justice Sid Clark ruled there was sufficient evidence to take Gurmit Singh Dhillon to trial on a charge of first-degree murder. Clark set a date of February 6, 1998, in the provincial court in Nanaimo to fix a trial date. The judge then ordered a change of venue to the Supreme Court in Victoria. On February 16, Dhillon's trial was set to begin on November 3. At this point, the trial was expected to last four to six weeks. That would later increase to nine weeks.

That same month, Arid Lacis, the electron microscopy specialist with RCMP E Division, received Exhibit 26, the vacuum cleaner bag containing the results of the initial police examination of Dhillon's Blazer. Lacis was asked to examine and compare the contents of the bag with the dirt from the jacket (Exhibit 27). In particular, he was asked to examine the contents of the bag to determine if there were any beads similar to Particle no. 8—the single tiny iron bead—or the nineteen carbonaceous particles from the jacket. Microscopic examination of an extract from Exhibit 26 revealed fifty-one particles described as "dark beads." Those beads, although not identical to the single iron bead and the nineteen carbon particles from the footprint on Carolyn's jacket, were found to be "very similar" in their surface features and chemical composition to those found in Dhillon's Blazer two weeks after the crime.

MEANWHILE, AS THE two-year anniversary of the Jessica States murder approached, Dan Smith provided local media with an update of the investigation to date. Speaking to the *Alberni Valley Times* on July 22, Smith noted that the nature of the killing was so horrific that even hardened sex offenders had come forward voluntarily to submit blood samples for DNA testing. Those who did not come forward were sampled under a DNA warrant, he later added. "We've spoken to 4,890 subjects and we've built 3,640 case files," Smith said. "We have 871 (evidence) exhibits and we've received 968 tips." The investigator confirmed that there had been rumours about possible suspects. However, since the killing, there had been several suicides involving men who were identified as living in the community at the time of the killing. Smith said those suspects had been DNA sampled postmortem—and clearly ruled out.

To date, police had collected 348 blood samples from "persons of interest" or males who were in the vicinity at the time of the crime. As of July 6, 1997, those samples had been processed on a priority basis, Smith noted, adding that he was still tracking down individuals from whom to obtain samples. Here Smith raised the point about the genetic anomaly Hiron Poon had observed in the suspect DNA profile, and which had initially led investigators to believe he was of non-Caucasian, possibly black/African, heritage. "We know the killer has a unique DNA stamp—something our lab people haven't seen before," he said, "But we don't have any science which would tell us what characteristics this might produce."

Smith said forensic investigators had also collected hair samples from the crime scene. While there was no way to be sure if the evidence came from the suspect for certain, those samples had been sent to the US Army lab in Maryland for mitochondrial DNA analysis. While the hair root contains the complete DNA profile of the donor, mitochondrial DNA found in the hair fibre provides only the DNA profile of the donor's mother (known as matrilineal DNA). The US Army had pioneered mitochondrial DNA analysis and technology, mainly for the purpose of identifying bodies, and now offered the service to law enforcement. Even today, it is considered useful in determining maternally linked relationships and can prove helpful in identifying a suspect pool or a burned corpse, but it is not considered conclusive in a court of law. Smith said the RCMP had spent about $40,000 on mitochondrial DNA testing.

That same day, Stefano Mazzega provided the *Times* with an update on the changeover to PCR technology at the E Division's forensic lab. Mazzega advised that since the time of Jessica's murder, the RCMP had advanced two full generations in DNA technology. The first samples had been tested using the original RFLP process, then retested using the first generation of PCR technology, which was fully installed by September 1997. "We've changed to a refinement of PCR technology," Mazzega told the *Times*. "Originally, we could study three or four loci (gene structures) per gel—now we can study nine. It's called a Nineplex, and it's now commercially available."

Under the original technology, it was possible to exclude a suspect with a single gel. However, in order to make a ten-loci match, it was necessary to run at least three separate tests. The Nineplex process had the potential to speed up the processing of samples, but would require about six months of testing, Mazzega said.

DHILLON GOES TO TRIAL

The trial of Gurmit Singh Dhillon opened in *voir dire* (no jury present) on Tuesday, November 3, 1998, in the Supreme Court in Victoria. The jury—eight women and four men—had been selected the previous day. But on opening day, Dhillon's counsel, Russ Chamberlain, and senior Crown counsel Darrill Prevett advised Justice Al Stewart that they would present evidence out of the presence of the jury for the first three days of the trial. Chamberlain set the tone for the trial during the *voir dire* session. Spectators were allowed, as were reporters, but Chamberlain stipulated that they could not report on the proceedings themselves. Brian Wilford, a staff reporter for the *Alberni Valley Times*, covered the trial. He wrote, "Mr. Dhillon, balding, silvering, and wearing glasses, was dressed in a black suit. He sat quietly through the proceedings. When he was released from custody on

$250,000 bail, he was ordered to live with his sister in Nanoose Bay. Neither members of his family nor the Lee family attended Tuesday's proceedings."

As the investigator who had advanced the case forward through evolving DNA law and technology (and file coordinator), Dan Smith became the focal point of Chamberlain's attack on the evidence and police procedure. "So much of the evidence that would point to a conviction hinged on the jury hearing the grounds for the DNA warrant. That was very vigorously defended," Smith said. "As with all murders, it was a very complex case that stretched out over a long period of time, so it was very vigorously defended and very accusatory in tone. In other words, any little perceived thing that they could point to, to indicate a Charter violation, they certainly did."

Smith noted that, early in the investigation, it felt like the goalposts provided by the Charter of Rights and Freedoms were still actively evolving. But by late 1998, a number of key Charter precedents had been established. It was during the *voir dire* that Justice Stewart threw out the consent sample. Now, because the overwhelming odds had been calculated by compounding the profiles produced using both the consent and warranted samples, the DNA case was at risk.

"Certainly, it was disheartening," says Smith, "and certainly, I didn't want to be responsible for a Charter violation that would result in this multi-year investigation being wasted." But by now, Prevett had located a private lab in the Vancouver suburb of Richmond that did PCR analysis. With the balance of the trial now at risk, Smith made the first of two fast trips to the Lower Mainland.

By November 1998, PCR technology had improved markedly, along with the turnaround time. "I took the sample to the lab in Richmond, and they did the analysis on the weekend. It cost the Crown $10,000, and on Monday morning we were back in court with odds of one in 165 million. The science had progressed so much that they were able to accomplish in two days what it had taken us years to do during the course of the investigation." The trial opened before the jury on Monday, November 9.

LYLE PRICE, CALLED as a witness for the Crown, said he cannot recall exactly when he was advised that, twenty-one years after the fact, he would be asked to relate the exact details of that wet day in the potato field, and then face aggressive cross-examination by a well-known and formidable defence attorney. "Somebody phoned me up and asked me if I could be in Victoria for a while," he recalled. "I said I'd go—I'd testify. Of course, they prepped me before [testifying] and asked me some questions." The coaching included how to handle himself during cross-examination. "They tell you, don't answer anything that isn't asked. It wasn't rocket science. It was an interesting process, but a lot of waiting around. Of course, it would have been absolutely fascinating to have been in the courtroom the whole time, but you can't do that."

And that raised one question that lingers. Typically, after a witness testifies, they are allowed to attend the remaining proceedings, but Price was required to leave the courtroom. Price said he believes the Crown wanted to keep him in reserve for additional testimony, but he never returned to the stand.

In his opening remarks, David Kidd, the Crown counsel from Port Alberni, told jurors it had taken twenty years before DNA science had evolved to the stage where it could provide a match for the small and degraded samples retained by investigators in 1977. Kidd expressed his confidence that after hearing the DNA evidence, in combination with other evidence and witness testimony, the jurors would "have little difficulty concluding that Gurmit Singh Dhillon committed this crime," as Wilford reported.

Kidd recounted the recreation of Carolyn's last walk from the dance studio and the route that should have seen her arrive at her parent's restaurant just minutes later. He then described Dhillon's projected route from the nearby Alberni Foundry. Kidd spelled out the physical evidence that was collected at the time of the crime, with a brief outline of the improvements in technology, and the new laws created to allow police and prosecutors to use and to present DNA evidence under Canadian law.

On November 10, Sergeant Donald Blair, former head of the Port Alberni General Investigation Section and former lead investigator on the case, took the stand to testify on the early days of the investigation. Blair gave a steady and full account of the nineteen-hour search that ensued after his watch commander called him at home at 9:15 PM on the night Carolyn was reported missing: "But the white-haired retired officer's voice caught, then dropped to a whisper when his testimony came to 4:15 PM April 15, 1977. The call came in from the watch commander telling him 'the missing girl has been discovered.' With the courtroom hushed, he paused and looked down for a few moments to collect himself, pushing back obvious pain from more than two decades ago."

Sixteen years after the trial, in an extended telephone interview with me, Blair's memory was no less detailed and, at key points, no less emotional than his testimony before the jury. Under cross-examination, defence counsel Russ Chamberlain emphasized that his client had been fully cooperative when police asked to examine his truck, noting that "no warrants were necessary." Blair conceded that there was no direct evidence to disprove the alibi Dhillon had provided in his initial interview. But within the time sequence Dhillon outlined—his departure from the foundry between 6:30 and 7:00 PM, the trip through the free car wash, and beers at the Beaufort Hotel—Blair emphasized that there was a critical gap of at least a half hour, if not more.

Blair told the court he had timed himself driving from the most likely site where Carolyn would have been abducted to the abandoned railway siding where her body was found. With a driving time of five minutes each way, he maintained that the crime could have been accomplished in that critical half-hour gap. He conceded that the first bulletins he sent out to other police departments incorrectly stated that the tires on the suspect's vehicle were possibly 750 x 16 or 750 x 17 Seiberlings and that the front tires may have been ribbed summer-tread tires, despite the conclusion of Jack Mackenzie, owner of Jack's Tire, that the tires were definitely the smaller 700 x 15 Seiberlings. Mackenzie would later testify that he had no idea why police had considered the larger tires in their search.

AFTER A ONE-DAY break for the Remembrance Day holiday, Chamberlain ramped up the pressure in his cross-examination of Blair, suggesting that Dhillon was "another Guy Paul Morin." (In that infamous case, Morin was wrongfully convicted, in 1992, of the murder of a child, Christine Jessop. After DNA analysis of the evidence, Morin was cleared of the murder in 1995, and an inquiry into the case by the province of Ontario concluded that police had skewed evidence to secure a conviction.)

While Chamberlain cited the DNA evidence as incontestable proof of Morin's innocence, he would later contend vigorously that the new technology was fallible and of little worth in proving his client's guilt. Chamberlain accused the RCMP of conducting their investigation with "tunnel vision," after establishing the link with Dhillon's tire treads. He said police "only considered information to convict."

In his testimony, Ian MacDonald, the constable who had worked on the sexual assault case of Mildred Rose Mickey around the same time as Carolyn Lee was murdered, explained how Mickey had identified Dhillon's vehicle. Chamberlain then pounced on the fact that, during the subsequent photo lineup, Mickey had unhesitatingly excluded Dhillon as her attacker. "As a last-ditch effort to nail him, you pointed him out to her," Chamberlain said. "You were trying to get Dhillon at all costs, to the point where you were willing to throw out your integrity as a police officer." Chamberlain said that the theme of the investigation was "get Dhillon." Chamberlain would maintain this stance throughout the trial, as well as bringing into question the reliability of DNA technology and analysis.

Dan Smith took the stand the next day. During questioning from Prevett, the investigator placed into evidence numerous bagged items that had been collected at the crime scene twenty-one years earlier:

> one pair of light blue panties bristling with red and white identification tags

> a jade green sweater with dark-green and orange stripes

> white leotards

> various swabs and samples

> hair samples from Carolyn, from her parents, and from
the accused

At this point, Chamberlain interjected that the samples also included hair that appeared to be blond. One item seemed to have special significance, although it was not revealed at the time: "Blue jeans in a box wrapped in brown paper and all of that in a plastic bag. Just back from the lab in Vancouver last week, said Corporal Smith, without saying why," as Wilford reported.

What the court never heard was that the jeans worn by Carolyn had caused another mad scramble for analysis, a hasty round-trip to the Lower Mainland for Dan Smith, and a career highlight for one Vancouver cab driver. When Smith first began his testimony in the *voir dire* hearing the previous week, he spotted something he had not previously noticed in the evidence.

"The exhibits had been seized in 1977. I had gone through them, but I had not examined them physically," Smith said. "It would have been pointless for me to do that because I am not an analyst. So there I am at trial, handing over exhibits in bags. Naturally, I was wearing rubber gloves when I handed over a pair of jeans. As I was doing that, I noticed a white stain on the leg of the jeans. I pointed this out to Prevett, who immediately asked for an adjournment.

"I phoned the lab. I had gone over the exhibit and noted they had not found any biological material on them. Nonetheless, there, staring at me, was a white stain on the leg. I asked if they could do a scan on this if I flew over there right away, and they said yes." Smith rushed down to Harbour Air, where there was a floatplane waiting to take him to Vancouver. Along the way, he arranged for a taxi to be waiting at the dock.

"I got in the taxi and explained, 'I am a policeman. I have to get to the RCMP lab at 37th and Heather, and I have to get there as quickly as possible because I am in the middle of a trial.'" Naturally, the cabbie was sceptical and Smith had to assure him this wasn't some sort of trap. "I told him, 'I'm not going to give you a ticket. I'm a murder investigator, not a traffic cop.'" Smith promised to wave his badge if they were pulled over by the Vancouver City Police. The cab driver told him, "'I've waited for this moment my whole life,' and off he went like a shot, driving like a maniac. He got me to the lab in no time, and as we were pulling up, I told him it would be about twenty minutes to get the lab work done and could he arrange to have another taxi to get me back to the floatplane? He said, 'I'll wait for you.'"

Disappointingly, the white stain had no evidentiary value, so it was a wasted trip, but it demonstrated how far the Crown was willing to go to bring in a successful prosecution in this prototype case. Smith said one only had to look back at the 1995 murder trial of former NFL star O.J. Simpson to learn how not to prosecute a case that turned on DNA evidence. While investigator Mark Fuhrman's mishandling of the notorious "bloody glove" was the most glaring flaw in the prosecution's case, Los Angeles police technicians and lab scientists also made a succession of procedural errors while gathering state's evidence, making Simpson's acquittal almost inevitable. "We were somewhat better off in that we were not dealing with the American style of justice," said Smith, "and we were well aware of the need to maintain continuity of exhibits and of all manner of techniques required to prevent contamination of exhibits. That was one of the major concerns in the O.J. case."

AFTER LAYING OUT the Crown's case before the jury, Smith faced another round of cross-examination from Chamberlain. This time, the defence counsel pulled out all the stops. "He was very vigorous in defending his client. Every question had an accusatory tone to it. You always felt like you were the accused. You're definitely under attack, here. That played along for quite a while. I believe, at one point, David Kidd objected, and the judge agreed. I can't even remember what the question was. I was just thankful that someone came along and said, 'Enough's enough!'"

Smith said he was well aware of Chamberlain's reputation as anti-police and "a bit of a dragon" in court. While taking the brunt of Chamberlain's courtroom fury, Smith said that he could appreciate that Chamberlain was an effective defence lawyer. "Mr. Dhillon certainly got a very good defence—the best defence that he could have hoped for," he said. All told, Smith spent four days on the stand in the Dhillon trial, about half of that in cross-examination by Chamberlain. "Chamberlain was all over me as I defended the DNA warrant. He was on me like a pit bull on a poodle."

At the end of Chamberlain's cross-examination, however, Smith and Prevett were satisfied that Chamberlain had not been able to poke any holes in the chain of evidence. Still, there was always the possibility of an appeal, and if the appeal court overturned the validity of the 1996 DNA warrant, the Crown would be forced to call for a retrial. But by now, the higher courts had upheld the use of cast-off DNA evidence, and Smith saw his opportunity to collect a sample as the trial progressed. In the lobby of the Victoria courthouse, next to the sheriff's office, was a coffee kiosk with a bench situated adjacent to the front door.

"It's first thing in the morning, and I'm sitting there having a coffee. I look outside the glass door, and there is Gurmit Dhillon having a cigarette with his sister. He puts out the cigarette in the ashtray, right in front of me, then walks in through the door past me, sneering at me." Smith happened to be carrying his briefcase, which contained, along with notebooks, all manner of evidence-gathering materials.

"I open my briefcase, take out a pair of gloves and an exhibit bag, walk outside, and take the one and only cigarette butt that's in this ashtray—it's a sand-type ashtray. I put it in the exhibit bag, seal the exhibit bag, mark it with date, time, and initials, and put it in my briefcase. I take off my rubber gloves.

"The deputy sheriff witnessed all of this, and he was smiling because he had clearly clued in to what I was doing. I threw my gloves in the wastepaper basket and got my notebook out. I started to write notes about gathering the cigarette butt and felt pretty proud of myself because, if this case went to appeal, we wouldn't need to rely on [the warranted sample] because now I had a cast-off DNA sample as well.

Then I looked up, and Mr. Chamberlain was hovering over me. He said to me, 'I see what you're doing,' thinking I was backdating my notes or something, not realizing I was making current notes about a seizure I'd just made from his client."

Once again, the effort proved to be unnecessary, but working on a prosecution so fraught with precedents, no one wanted to lose this case on a point of procedure. Well after the consent sample got thrown out, but after the Richmond testing brought the odds back up, Smith said it was merely a contingency. "I now know I can do this. And if there is an appeal, and the appeal is successful, and a new trial is ordered, I now have DNA from Dhillon that will be admissible."

LYLE PRICE WOULD also face Russ Chamberlain on cross-examination. But the defence attorney would discover that this was one confident, articulate (former) potato farmer. Despite his place in the chain of evidence, however, Price says he did not figure significantly in the Crown's case—at least, not based on the amount of time on the stand. "I was [in Victoria] for quite some time, but I didn't testify for very long," he said. "They went over the details of finding [Carolyn]. Then I got cross-examined on, 'How did I know it was a four-wheel drive vehicle that was in there?'"

Eighteen years later, Price still reflects the exasperation of having had to spell out the obvious to a questioner who did not appear to have any knowledge on the subject. "He said, 'So how did you know it was a four-wheel drive? It could have been any vehicle.' I said, 'Well, it was pretty muddy; it had traction tires all around.' The four tires were traction-lug, because you could tell where they turned in the mud. I said, 'Obviously, it would have spun if it hadn't been an all-wheel or four-wheel drive type vehicle, because it was that slippery. It had been mixed rain and snow that night, and it was wet down there.'"

Price said that, at that point, unable to establish much in the way of doubt as to the identity of the suspect vehicle, Chamberlain shut down the cross-examination. "He said, 'Oh!' and basically dismissed me," Price said. "He didn't want to get into it any further."

The photographic and plaster cast evidence of the tire tracks were especially clear because of the mud and the fact that there was a bit of an incline that caused the heavy tires to dig deeply and leave a clear impression, Price explained. The chances of a two-wheel-drive vehicle being mounted with heavy-lug tires all around were pretty much zero. It was a low-percentage line of questioning, and Chamberlain obviously didn't want to waste a lot of time, he said.

ON FRIDAY, NOVEMBER 13, the forensic pathologist, Dr. Rex Ferris, took to the stand. In 1988, after learning about the new science of forensic DNA, Dan Smith had contacted Ferris, who was considered Canada's leading expert. Ferris advised the court that the autopsy of Carolyn Lee on April 16, 1977, had been performed by Dr. Robert Clark, who'd died the previous February. The pathologist recounted in excruciating detail the massive damage inflicted on Carolyn's young body during the savage attack. The November 16 headline in the *Alberni Valley Times* was no less graphic: "Carolyn Lee Likely Face Down When Fatal Blows Dealt." Ferris testified that two and "probably more" blows were delivered to the back of the girl's skull while she lay face down in the mud. "The blows shattered a twelve-centimetre hole in her skull, he said, and caused a fracture down to the top of her spine."

Ferris testified that, while it was possible the damage was caused by kicks from a steel-toed work boot, he believed it was more likely that the assailant used an object such as a tire iron or a rock. "Her assailant would almost certainly have been splattered with blood and brain matter, he said."

A scrape on Carolyn's right thigh indicated she had been dragged over a sharp edge—likely a rock—while she was still alive. Ferris testified that Carolyn was raped before she died, and likely survived for as long as thirty minutes after she was beaten. If that were indeed the case, according to the timeline established by Dhillon, the accused was already back in town, drinking a beer, while the child drew her final agonized breaths in the muddy potato field.

MONDAY, NOVEMBER 16, was Gurmit Dhillon's forty-eighth birthday. On that day, his ex-wife, Sharon McLeod, took the stand. McLeod testified that, although the police conducted a search of her home immediately after Dhillon's Blazer and its tire tracks were linked to the crime scene, police did not interview her. When police arrived with a warrant, McLeod was alone in the house but waited outside during the search that included seizing her vacuum cleaner bags.

McLeod testified that she did not give a statement to police until November 26, 1983, after she had separated from the accused. McLeod then recounted the sequence in which, after Dhillon did not arrive home by 6:30 PM, she drove to several bars to try to locate him before returning home and seeing him drive past on Third Avenue at about 6:45. The jury now heard what she had first told police fifteen years previously.

In a cross-examination that extended into the next day, Chamberlain vigorously attacked McLeod's credibility, accusing her of "putting together this story out of vengeance on your husband." Calling it "gilded evidence" and "fake evidence," the defence counsel attempted to break McLeod's composure. "I say you've made the whole story up," he suggested.

"That's not correct," McLeod answered calmly. Noting discrepancies between her trial testimony and her 1983 statement to police, Chamberlain pointed out that she didn't mention phoning the Beaufort Hotel or driving there, that she didn't tell police she saw her husband drive past, heading toward Ship Creek Road, and that she didn't mention finding an earring in the Blazer. "That's correct," she replied, equally calmly. When Chamberlain pointed out that, at the time of her statement, she said she did not know whether the mud she washed off the Blazer came from the foundry, she replied simply, "That's true."

Chamberlain kept the pressure up on the second day of his cross-examination. Pointing out that McLeod testified that she knew Dhillon was a suspect in the Lee killing, he suggested that she must have been "a brutal monster" to have brought her daughter and two younger sons to live in his house. "That's not correct," she replied. "I simply didn't believe he was the killer." McLeod said she soon discovered that Dhillon was a hard drinker and a womanizer and that she would regularly make calls to local bars looking for him. And she also began to collect jewellery off the floor of his truck.

McLeod testified that on the day she first spoke to police, she actually went to the detachment to speak to speak to officers about one of her sons who was involved with a youth gang. But while she was there, the conversation turned to her estranged husband and his possible involvement in the Lee murder. That visit turned into a marathon. McLeod first arrived at the detachment at two in the afternoon, and subsequently spoke to then-GIS head Sergeant Bob Martin. She did not leave the detachment until 8:40 that evening.

Once again, Chamberlain accused her of fabricating the entire story. "You were mad at Gurmit," he said. "You made up this story to cause trouble for him."

"That's not correct," McLeod replied. Chamberlain then suggested that Sergeant Martin and the other officers colluded with her at length to put together an elaborate sequence of events for her statement.

That was a charge that Martin refuted when he took the stand following McLeod. He did concede that her statement, which ran to thirty-eight pages, would not have consumed the five hours that ensued after he took over the interview in mid-afternoon. Martin said there was likely a break in between, but it was not part of the written record.

ON NOVEMBER 19, Anne-Elizabeth Charland took the stand to testify that the material taken from the body of Carolyn Lee matched blood samples collected from Gurmit Singh Dhillon. Charland, like Stefano Mazzega, was a reporting officer, but she was based in the biology section of the RCMP's forensic laboratory in Ottawa. She began her testimony with a recounting of the long and at times frustrating sequence in which the crime scene evidence samples were successively tested for DNA.

Charland testified that an "analyst" [Hiron Poon] also took DNA samples from Carolyn's parents, John and Sau Lee, to recreate Carolyn's DNA pattern and "build a family tree in reverse order." (Eight months later, Dan Smith asked Poon to use the same strategy to establish a genetic family tree in the Jessica States investigation. But in this instance, it was the suspect's parents, rather than the victim's, that were sampled covertly.) Charland further noted that, despite the poor results yielded by the early DNA tests, an Esquimalt man had been eliminated as the mysterious "second suspect" because his DNA profile differed markedly from the genetic material collected at the scene. As soon as one comparison point does not match, it is considered "an exclusion," she explained. But "there were no exclusions" in the 1996 test of Gurmit Singh Dhillon. The match was so good that the analysts considered it "a rare event."

Charland testified to the effectiveness of the new PCR technology used to analyze the five large swabs collected at the crime scene in 1977 and preserved for years by the investigators. According to Charland, the RFLP process required 500 billionths of a gram of genetic material to produce a DNA profile; the latest PCR technology required just one billionth of a gram. To process the material on the vaginal swabs, scientists first had to remove the bacterial DNA from the human DNA, then the female DNA of the victim (hence the reconstructed DNA profile of Carolyn) from the DNA belonging to the suspect—or suspects. The resulting male DNA profile was then compared to the DNA from the warranted sample from Dhillon.

In his cross-examination the next day, Chamberlain attacked both the credibility of forensic science and the integrity of the scientists who performed it. The defence counsel told the jury that the Crown was asking them to convict a man of first-degree murder based on "something we can't see." He said to Charland, "We've got to trust you to convict this man. You knew Dhillon was a suspect. 'Get Dhillon' was what your mission was."

"I have no mission of that sort, no," Charland replied. Chamberlain then cited a DNA request written by investigators that appeared to advise her to find a link to Gurmit Dhillon while at the same time excluding the second suspect identified in 1989. Charland conceded that the wording was inappropriate, but, "It doesn't matter anyway; I depend on the results."

Chamberlain attacked the results of any test that analyzed "degraded" or "rotted" material. On this point, Charland was adamant: degraded samples might not produce a DNA profile, but there was no science to indicate that they could produce inaccurate profiles. "If you get a profile, it's a true profile," she said.

Chamberlain then ran the witness through an extended review of the lab and the equipment used or worn by scientists. The focus on scientific minutiae led Justice Stewart to interrupt Charland's testimony several times. "I don't know about the jury, but using myself as a common denominator—I'm lost," he observed. Chamberlain continued to demand detailed explanations of the procedures, and Charland kept returning to the central theme of her testimony throughout: four pairs of coded peaks on the crime scene samples that exactly matched four coded peaks on Dhillon's warranted blood sample. And no exclusions.

Chamberlain found a little more currency in his contention of procedural error in his cross-examination of Richard Guerrieri, the scientist who worked at Roche Biomedical Labs in North Carolina at the time the lab received the Carolyn Lee samples. By the time of the trial, Guerrieri was a forensic biological examiner for the FBI and considered one of the world's top experts in forensic DNA. In 1993, he opened the package of samples from Genelex Corporation in Seattle containing swabs, hair, and blood samples. At that time, Roche Biomedical had PCR technology that was superior to that used by both Genelex and the RCMP's central forensic lab in Ottawa. Guerrieri testified that he identified five DNA sites, wrote his report, and returned the sample package to the RCMP in September 1994. In Ottawa, one of the analysts subsequently discovered that some of the hair samples labelled as belonging to Dhillon actually belonged to the "second suspect." Guerrieri testified that the labelling mistake had been made at the Genelex lab and that, once the labelling mistake was noted, his company notified the RCMP lab. That was in early 1995.

Chamberlain pointed out that, in two instances, the Roche report contained two incorrect notations, indicating that DNA samples had been tested when they hadn't. Guerrieri explained that the lab did mix up the labelling of two sample extracts. "Yes sir. That was an error—a transcription error," Guerrieri said. Chamberlain maintained that this error had caused confusion for his DNA experts, who were unable to find the corresponding test results. In response, Guerrieri noted that the mislabelled samples were not used to produce results in the Dhillon case.

On Tuesday, November 23, a population geneticist, Dr. Richard Carmody of Carleton University, testified that the chances that any man other than Gurmit Dhillon had sex with Carolyn Lee were one in 165 million. "I think most of us would agree a number like that is pretty rare," Carmody observed, because it meant that "99.9999994 percent of the population would not have that profile." Carmody testified that by compiling the results of the testing by Ottawa RCMP, Genelex, and Roche Biomedical, along with those from Helix Biotech, the result of Dan Smith's rush trip to Vancouver on November 8, scientists had put together a "ten-area match." Further, Dhillon was not excluded by any of the match points, the scientist explained. The odds were calculated using a database of Caucasians because, as Carmody explained, Indo-Canadian people are often considered Caucasian in genetic terms.

The next day, Dr. Ranajit Chakraborty from the University of Texas expanded on the racial sub-groups within the nominally Caucasian population. Chakraborty, another population geneticist, was the scientist Prevett had contacted after Dan Smith speculated that combining the early meagre DNA results from separate laboratories might provide a better exclusionary result. It was Chakraborty, using the "product rule," who had calculated odds of one in 165 million, using the Caucasian population. However, the scientist explained, using a population base composed entirely of Punjabi Sikh men, those odds fell to one in 13.3 million. Given a population base of Indians as a non-homogenous, composite population with sub-groups, that number could fall to as low as one in 7.6 million, he further explained. If Punjabi Sikhs were considered a homogenous population, the odds rose to fourteen million to one, but as a composite population with sub-groups, it was one in 13.3 million, he said. That excluded 99.9999925 percent of Punjabi Sikh men as donors.

In his cross-examination, Chamberlain pointed out that, in 1997, the Crown based its case on an eight-loci match, which produced odds of two million to one, then subsequently claimed that amazing ten-loci match and the one in 165 million odds. Chamberlain told Chakraborty that his DNA expert would testify that the jump from eight loci to ten was invalid because those additional two DNA loci were not verified as independent from other, testable DNA locations on the human genome. At this suggestion, Chakraborty countered that Chamberlain's DNA expert had fallen behind the times. Not only had those two specific additional loci since been identified as independent (which would allow analysts to compound the odds), but scientists had now identified another two dozen loci on the human genome that could be tested for DNA matches.

In previous testimony, Richard Carmody had testified that in 1996, Genelex had made an error in a DNA suit involving a paternity case. Chamberlain had told Carmody that his expert would testify that the error rate in DNA match is one in 1,000. To that contention, Carmody said that tossing around a facile "error rate" was improper procedure. "The error rate in this case is zero," he had concluded.

Chakraborty concurred. "From examining the material, I don't see any possibility of error," he said. At this point, Justice Stewart cautioned the jury not to attach too much significance to the numbers, suggesting that statistics often amount to "pious fraud." Stewart instead suggested that jurors pay more attention to the experts' interpretation of those numbers, such as "very uncommon" or "rare." On that point Chakraborty agreed, terming the results of the Dhillon profile as "very uncommon."

THE DEFENCE MAKES ITS CASE

On Thursday, November 26, forensic engineer Jason Gough, of Vancouver-based Baker Engineering, took to the stand on behalf of the defence. Gough testified that he'd been hired by the defence to reconstruct the timeline of the crime as alleged by the Crown using the accused as a live prop.

On September 17, 1998, Dhillon was asked to work a full day at Alberni Foundry, wearing clothes similar to those he had worn in the spring of 1977. At about 4:30 PM, Gough testified, a "very dirty" Dhillon washed his hands and left the foundry, as he told police he had done on the day of the crime. Gough and Dhillon then drove to the site of the old foundry at the foot of Second Avenue, where he gave Dhillon a mannequin dressed in clothes similar to those Carolyn Lee wore on the last day of her life—a nylon ski jacket, blue jeans, black body suit, blue panties, and white running shoes. The mannequin was dressed in a sweatshirt instead of a green sweater and grey leotards instead of white. With a video camera running, Dhillon and Gough drove to Third Avenue and Athol, where it was believed Carolyn was abducted. From there, they proceeded along Third Avenue to Ship Creek Road and continued onto Franklin River Road to the wooded area near the abandoned railway siding where Lee's body was found.

Gough testified that he left the camera running as he asked Dhillon to take the mannequin out of the car and lay it on the ground where the body was found. At this point, on prompting, Dhillon undressed the mannequin. He was then asked to step on the back of the jacket, then walk approximately seventy-five paces and back to step on it again, leaving two footprints similar to those found on the jacket taken from the crime scene. When that was complete, Dhillon and Gough scattered the clothes along the shore of Cox Lake.

Judge Stewart cleared the courtroom of spectators and media prior to playing the ten-minute video presentation. Gough testified that he then took the clothes back to Vancouver where, on the weekend of October 3 through 6, he laid them out on the roof of Baker Engineering. That weekend, seventeen millimetres of rain fell, which, he testified, was similar to the eighteen millimetres of mixed rain and snow that fell in the Alberni Valley between the estimated time of Lee's death on April 14, 1977, and 4:50 PM on April 15, when her body was found.

Gough testified that he then brought the clothes inside to dry and subjected them to an examination for particles, first using a visual inspection, then a regular microscope followed by an electron microscope with an X-ray analyzer. His conclusions cut straight to the heart of Chamberlain's defence. The defence counsel had cross-examined successive witnesses as to the condition of Lee's clothing at the time her body was discovered. How, he asked, could a dirty foundry worker forcibly remove her clothes without leaving foundry residues—carbon, coke, coal, aluminium, or silicon? Gough's testimony backed up that argument. The engineer said he found smudge marks on the sweatshirt, jeans, jacket, and tights. All contained carbon, aluminium, and silicon residues. "It was virtually impossible not to transfer foundry material to the clothing," he said. Under cross-examination by Prevett, however, Gough admitted that he did not factor in the possibility that a second assailant—the man in the back seat of the Blazer cited by Crown witness Alice Lazorko—may have removed Lee's clothing or that Lee, under extreme duress, had removed them herself.

Smith was not in court for the re-enactment video. He was asked whether, had the re-enactment exercise failed to support the defence case, the Crown would have been able to subpoena the video. "No. The onus is completely on the Crown to disclose. There is no necessity for the defence to disclose except in a Charter argument. So if the defence intends to raise a Charter argument, they have to disclose how they are going to do that."

Following the re-enactment presentation, DNA expert Dr. Vanora Kean, also testifying for the defence, said tests performed on the vaginal swabs taken from the crime scene consistently revealed genetic material from a second male. Kean told the jury that, until March 1998, she was the forensic supervisor at Genelex, where the first PCR analysis was performed, yielding a single loci match (site DQ Alpha) with Dhillon. However, Kean testified, there were also indicators of another contributor in the Genelex sample. Kean further said that when she examined the tests performed by the RCMP Central Laboratory, she found "one unusual feature" in a test that had been discarded by RCMP analyst Anne-Elizabeth Charland.

"Using the RCMP's own criteria, I would have said the results are 'inconclusive' or there is evidence of additional data," Kean said. "Additional data" would indicate DNA from another source—in short, another suspect. In his appeal application, Chamberlain would later raise that issue, but the "DNA soup theory," as it was later tagged, was thoroughly discredited by the scientists.

A second defence expert, Laurence Mueller, a professor in the Department of Ecology and Evolutionary Biology at the University of California at Irvine, told the court that there were two methods of estimating the odds on a DNA match, the counting method and the product rule. Mueller testified that while the Crown experts had used the product rule to calculate their odds in the tens of millions to one, he had employed the "more conservative" counting method, which yielded a probability of one in 582. Mueller subsequently admitted that the counting method "is not generally accepted within his scientific community," and that the product rule was used by most government and research laboratories in North America. In Canada, the product rule was endorsed by the National Research Council. The scientist also agreed that a ten-loci match between unrelated individuals was "very uncommon," and he had never seen it previously.

ON THE FINAL day of testimony, Friday, November 27, Dhillon took to the stand to tell the court he did not kill Carolyn Lee. Brian Wilford, the *Alberni Valley Times* reporter, described the forty-eight-year-old man as "silver-haired and balding," and noted that he "wore a black suit and a white shirt unbuttoned at the collar, as he has every day at the trial."

Dhillon testified in a low, measured voice and did not change his tone even when Chamberlain asked him flat out whether he had abducted or helped to abduct, rape, and murder Carolyn Lee. "No, I did not," he replied. In his testimony, which lasted less than an hour, even with cross-examination, Dhillon mainly recounted the facts as he had given in his police statement on April 26, 1977. He initially misstated the date of the murder as April 24, and testified that he first learned of her death on April 25. When brought to his attention, Dhillon amended his statement to reset the dates to April 14 and 15.

Most of the information Dhillon gave the jury was redundant: At the time of the crime, Dhillon owned a Chevy Blazer; he had purchased 700 x 15 Seiberling tires at Pearson Tire, and he worked for his father at Alberni Foundry. He described the scene after work on April 14, when two friends of his father showed up and all had several drinks. Dhillon testified that he was "very dirty" and used an air hose to blow loose dust from his clothing, grabbed his coat and lunchbox, locked the gate, and drove off between 6:30 and 7:00 PM. His time-line included two trips through the free car wash at Somass Division and beers at the Beaufort Hotel, and he named the same two contacts, Don McMurtry and bartender Ken Sherman. Dhillon also recounted the phone call from his wife, Sharon, and told the jury that when he left the bar at nine o'clock, she was waiting outside. She followed him home in her own car. He did not, he said, demand that she wash the Blazer, nor did he have a steering wheel cover to cut off.

Dhillon further said that Sharon's daughter, who was the same age as Carolyn Lee, lived in his home even after he became a suspect in the murder. Later, Sharon's sister moved in with them for a short time and brought her own eleven-year-old daughter. Dhillon also testified that he'd been upset by the re-enactment he was required to undertake with engineer Jason Gough.

With two of Carolyn Lee's sisters present in the courtroom, summations to the jury began on Monday, November 30. It became clear that Chamberlain believed his client's best chance of acquittal hinged on creating scepticism about forensic DNA and the scientists who practised it. Chamberlain told the jury that the DNA science linking his client to the crime was "a bunch of malarkey. The rest of the case supports the accused," Chamberlain said. "He has demonstrated his innocence."

In his later rebuttal, Prevett declared that the physical evidence and witness testimony were sufficient to place Dhillon in the area of both the abduction and the crime scene where Lee's body was found. Experts had testified that the DNA match to the suspect was "rare" or "very uncommon ... When you apply your good old-fashioned common sense to the totality of the evidence, you will be able to conclude beyond a reasonable doubt that the evidence is consistent with the accused committing this murder and inconsistent with any other rational explanation."

For his part, Chamberlain reminded jurors that "the greatest crime a democracy can commit is to convict innocent people." He then suggested that a guilty defendant would never have taken the stand to testify in his own defence as Dhillon had. "The accused is an innocent man. He didn't have to testify but he did—because he's innocent."

What Chamberlain didn't mention was that the "re-enactment" of the crime sequence as staged by engineer Jason Gough was likely the most critical piece of evidence the defence could bring to bear. And had the handling of the mannequin not yielded the result Chamberlain was seeking—copious amounts of foundry dust transferred to the "victim's" clothing—the resulting video would never have seen the light of day, much less be presented in the courtroom.

Re-emphasizing the alleged fixation of the RCMP on a single, convenient suspect, Chamberlain then dipped into popular culture, referencing a crime movie released three years previously. "I say it cuts to *Get Shorty*," he said, before repeating a central theme of the defence, "Let's get Dhillon." He cited the letter from the RCMP's central forensic laboratory, which a Crown witness had conceded was "inappropriate," that suggested police were focussed on matching Dhillon with DNA while eliminating the second suspect. "The lab owes its allegiance to the police. They were anxious to do the job: Get Dhillon."

Chamberlain again suggested that, by cooperating with police by giving a voluntary statement just twelve days after the crime, Dhillon had proven early on that he was innocent. He suggested that Dhillon's alibi was unshakable, and yet police continued to focus on him because of shaky evidence. "They worked themselves to the bone trying to disprove that alibi. Do you know what they came up with? Nothing."

Chamberlain dismissed as "patently ridiculous" the testimony of Dhillon's ex-wife, Sharon McLeod. "Her evidence is nothing more than [that of] a woman who wished to wreak her vengeance on a man." Chamberlain suggested it was extremely unlikely that Dhillon could have abducted a twelve-year-old girl and driven through the uptown core without being noticed. As for Alice Lazorko's testimony that she did indeed see Dhillon's blue Blazer pass by on Third Avenue with a Chinese girl in the back seat, Chamberlain called it "thoroughly unreliable," noting that her statement to police emphasized that a detailed memory of the event only sprang to mind in the context of a later, similarly horrifying homicide. To further discredit the witness, he noted that Lazorko was later hired on a part-time basis by Parksville RCMP.

Chamberlain also emphasized the initial police bulletin that misstated the tires mounted on the suspect vehicle. As for the footprint on Carolyn Lee's jacket containing carbonaceous material, Chamberlain conceded that it could have come from Alberni Foundry. But it could have come from any number of places, he noted. As for the DNA evidence, Chamberlain cautioned jurors to be "very, very suspicious." At this point he appeared to introduce some doublethink. "'Trust us'—this is the argument that is framed by these so-called experts. 'Trust us. We are the all-knowing scientists. We can decide who goes to jail,'" he told jurors. But in the same argument, Chamberlain suggested that jurors should trust the defence experts because his experts held doctorates while the Crown's DNA experts did not. That was a bit of a stretch; while the RCMP lab techs did not hold PhDs, the two Crown experts, Chakraborty and Carmody, both held doctoral degrees.

In his later rebuttal on that point, Prevett noted that Dr. Vanora Kean, the defence's DNA expert, had actually confirmed the DNA match with Dhillon while raising several issues of procedural error at one private lab that, in the end, proved to be irrelevant to the case. In the final analysis, Prevett said, one would have to conclude that the "very uncommon" ten-loci DNA match linking Dhillon to the genetic material on the vaginal swabs collected at the crime scene should lead to a finding of guilt.

Prevett maintained that the combination of physical evidence and witness testimony was sufficient to incriminate Dhillon. Perhaps more importantly, it had been sufficient grounds to obtain a DNA warrant under the law passed by Parliament in 1995. Even the timeline as presented by the defence provided the accused with enough time to commit the murder, Prevett emphasized.

The prosecutor defended the credibility of the two key witnesses who only came forward years later. Sharon McLeod may have married Dhillon, even knowing he was suspect in the crime, but her account of the evening of the crime was credible and not the fabrication of a vengeful ex-wife. "If she were out to get him, she could have said much more damaging things," Prevett suggested. That same logic applied to witness Alice Lazorko, he later noted. Her motivation was to find two killers, not to incriminate a man who had been a suspect for seventeen years. "If she were out to get the accused, why would she mention the blond man?"

Prevett then dismissed the videotaped "re-enactment" of the crime as "worthless," because it was based on too many assumptions— mainly that Dhillon himself had abducted, restrained, and undressed the victim, despite Alice Lazorko's testimony that a second man had restrained Lee in the back seat of the Blazer during the fatal drive to Cox Lake.

"Carolyn's death is first-degree murder because the evidence shows she was abducted as a prelude to her murder," Prevett concluded for the jury. "The totality of the case, beyond a reasonable doubt, is consistent with Gurmit Singh Dhillon committing the murder and inconsistent with any other conclusion."

In his instructions to the jury, Justice Al Stewart took pains to downplay the significance of DNA evidence in the Crown's case. "DNA evidence may establish nothing," Stewart maintained, as he warned the jury not to be "overwhelmed by the aura of scientific evidence."

Stewart's official scepticism notwithstanding, Chamberlain would maintain in his subsequent appeal of the guilty verdict that "the trial judge erred in not instructing the jury that the Crown's DNA evidence had no probative value [evidence which is sufficiently useful to prove something important in a trial] or, in the alternative, limited probative value, if they were not satisfied beyond a reasonable doubt that there was only one male donor to the DNA material taken from the vagina of the deceased."

While the issue of the potential second suspect would be a critical portion of the defence's grounds for appeal, the suggestion that the mix of genetic materials from two male donors could provide a hybrid DNA profile (the "DNA soup" theory) would later be dismissed out of hand by scientists. But in the meantime, Stewart's extended dissertation on the need for scepticism flew in the face of Chamberlain's contention that the judge had erred in his instructions.

In Stewart's statement to the jury before they sat down to begin their deliberations, he said: "Do not ever forget that, in dealing with the results of a DNA analysis placed before you by the Crown, you are, at the best, from the Crown's point of view, dealing with one piece of circumstantial evidence relevant to the identity of a perpetrator, nothing more. DNA profiling differs from earlier forms of identification evidence, such as analysis of blood and dental impressions, only in its increased power to discriminate between individuals ...

"Do not be overwhelmed by the aura of scientific infallibility associated with scientific evidence. DNA evidence is never, even on the Crown's best day, more than an item of circumstantial evidence. That is the best it can ever be, nothing more."

As is standard in jury briefings, Justice Stewart continued with a point-by-point definition of "reasonable doubt," and how it applies to both evidence and the credibility of witnesses. "If the evidence of the accused ... or of any of the witnesses placed before you by the accused, leaves you with a reasonable doubt as to his guilt, after considering it in the context of the whole of the evidence, then you must find the accused not guilty."

Stewart instructed that the jury had four basic options: They could find Dhillon not guilty of first-degree murder; they could find him guilty of first-degree murder; guilty of second-degree murder; or guilty of manslaughter. The first question they had to answer was, did

Dhillon assault Carolyn Lee? If not, they should proceed directly to a not-guilty verdict. If the answer was "yes," the next question to consider was whether the act was committed with reckless intent.

If the jury concluded that the act was not committed with reckless intent, they should find him guilty of manslaughter. But if it was, the next question was whether the reckless, intentional assault involved kidnapping or rape. If the answer was "no," the jury should bring in a guilty verdict on a charge of second-degree murder. If "yes," they should find him guilty of first-degree murder.

However, having spelled out the legal requirements for bringing in a guilty verdict in the three available options, Stewart advised that the only "realistic" verdicts in this specific case, which by definition involved abduction and sexual assault, were guilty or not guilty of first-degree murder. Stewart further advised that, legally speaking, the possibility of a second suspect was a red herring. "The accused only has to be party to the offence," he advised. "You can convict one even if the other has never been charged."

Once instructed, the jury began deliberating at 2:30 PM on Tuesday, December 1, and continued to deliberate until 9:40 PM. They resumed at 9:30 on Wednesday morning and would remain in deliberation until 9:45 that evening. But just before their lunch break on Wednesday, the jury foreman wrote a note to the judge: "My lord, may the jury hear the tape of the accused's testimony?" At two o'clock, following the lunch break, the jury filed back into the courtroom to hear the replay of Dhillon's testimony, which lasted approximately one hour.

THE VERDICT

At 5:25 PM on December 3, after three days of deliberations, the jury returned to Courtroom 302, having informed the sheriff they had reached a verdict. As the *Alberni Valley Times* reported, Dhillon sat facing straight ahead while waiting for the jurors to arrive. As they filed in, he appeared to be scanning their faces for telltale signs before the judge asked the familiar question.

"Mr. Foreman, have you reached a verdict?"

"Yes, my lord," the white-haired foreman replied.

"And what is your verdict?"

One word hung in the courtroom: "Guilty."

"Now let's get this straight. Guilty of what charge?" Stewart demanded.

"Guilty of first-degree murder, my lord," the foreman replied.

Stewart then asked all jurors who agreed with the verdict to stand. Twelve jurors rose to their feet.

"Some stared directly at Dhillon. He didn't flinch, didn't blink. He appeared to be in shock," reporter Brian Wilford wrote.

When asked by the judge whether he had anything to say, Dhillon hung his head for a long moment, before replying "No." Another pause. "Nothing to say."

Sentencing was brief and succinct. Justice Stewart delivered the mandatory sentence for conviction on first-degree murder: life in prison with no possibility of parole for twenty-five years. "Thank you," Stewart told the jury. "We'll simply adjourn."

At this point, Dhillon rose and placed his hands behind his back, waiting for the sheriff to arrive with the handcuffs. When the convicted man whispered a question to Chamberlain, the lawyer dismissed him. "There's nothing more to talk to me about," he said in voice loud enough to be heard throughout the courtroom. "We'll just have to talk to the family and see what we're going to do."

Lyle Price, who was standing in the doorway to the courtroom while the verdict was rendered, said the conversation resumed, more quietly this time. "He [Dhillon] asked, 'So what happens now?' And Chamberlain said, 'You go to jail.'"

ONE GUILTY PARTY was convicted of the crime, but the elusive blond second suspect has yet to be identified. All told, it had taken over twenty-one years to bring in a guilty verdict, although the appeal process would spin out for nearly three more years. The final decision took place two months after Port Alberni's other DNA case, the one involving Jessica States, wrapped up.

Dan Smith was at home when the guilty verdict came in. "I was awaiting a phone call with bated breath because this was my first big murder trial. In due course, I got a call that he was convicted. It was an unbelievable weight off my shoulders. The file was eleven years old when I got it, and ten more years [elapsed] before we got it to court ... I felt a huge sense of relief—first, that it was over and second, that the jury was able to see what I felt was the truth."

Smith said that he also felt a "sense of accomplishment because this was the first murder file that I had ever been assigned. And I had been assigned it not to solve it but to simply submit updates periodically. I'm not saying that I solved it, but I was part of the greater team that did. I was the primary investigator when it was solved."

What Smith wouldn't learn for some time was that, the same day Dhillon's conviction was announced in the December 4 edition of the *Alberni Valley Times*, Port Alberni RCMP arrested the killer of Jessica States. It would be eight months, however, before his voluntary DNA sample set off the alarm bells at RCMP headquarters.

Suspect on Ice

AT NOON ON December 4, 1998, the day after the jury found Gurmit Singh Dhillon guilty, Brian Wilford's story about the verdict appeared on the front page of the *Alberni Valley Times*: "Gurmit Singh Dhillon Guilty!"

The *Times* had made the transition to full digital production in July 1997, but the deadline ritual was much the same as the days when pages were cut, pasted, and photographed. For those who have never worked at a newspaper, "hot off the press" is just an abstract term. But in those days, it was a daily ritual. A bunch of reporters cranked out copy until eleven o'clock in the morning. After a quick edit, the copy was sent off to production. Production assembled the last news pages at deadline and sent them out to the RIP (raster image processor), where they were turned into full-size negatives, which were burned onto plates. The last plates were hung on the press and, soon enough, the entire building would begin to shake as the presses spooled up to operating speed.

And those bundles of newspapers heading out around noon were hot to the touch, as hot as the headline on the front page. It had taken twenty-one years, seven months, and nineteen days to bring Carolyn Lee's killer to justice. It was a heady moment to be part of that news team.

Also in the December 4, 1998, edition of the *Alberni Valley Times* was a letter to the editor from Corporal Dan Smith and Staff Sergeant Ken Williamson, second-in-command of the Port Alberni detachment, headlined "Surinder Dhillon Was Never a Suspect": "It has been brought to my attention that your media coverage of the trial in Monday's paper could be construed to portray [Gurmit Dhillon's brother] Surinder Singh Dhillon as a possible suspect in this murder." The article in question, said Smith and Williamson, had suggested that a defence witness made an out-of-context reference to Surinder Dhillon as a suspect. In their joint letter, Smith and Williamson explain that the brother of the accused voluntarily provided a DNA sample "as an investigation aide only, and there was never any reason for the police to suspect Surinder Dhillon of being involved in this crime." Meanwhile, the third Dhillon brother, Manjit, had readily stepped forward to be DNA sampled in the Jessica States blooding.

THAT DAY, I covered a series of events whose tentacles were to reach into the next DNA case in Port Alberni. First, I was called out in the morning to a recovery scene off River Road, where a woman had driven her car into the Somass River and required a swift-water rope rescue. Much to my annoyance, my trusty Nikon F-70 broke down, and I had to use my much slower backup camera, a Minolta Weathermatic. The slow action of this camera was to figure in a case later that day whose arrests set in motion the resolution of the murder of Jessica States.

That evening, the RCMP street crew, headed by Corporal Dave Finnen, collared a couple of otherwise ordinary young break-and-enter artists. Finnen had called me at home at about eight o'clock. "We're going to go out and bust down some doors tonight. Want to join us?" he asked. He explained that one of the two guys he arrested had ratted out his fence, who lived in the China Creek Apartments, about five blocks from my house. In the street crew's basement office at the RCMP detachment, the team suited up. Finnen handed me his bulletproof vest. "There may be firearms at the scene," he said. He knew how to sink the hook.

With warrant in hand, the crew took their places, guns drawn, at the suspect's door. I trailed behind, camera at the ready, knowing that, due to the slow cycling of the Weathermatic camera I had resorted to using that day, I was going to get one shot at a time. I hit the shutter as Constable Curtis Parker leaned back to put his foot through the apartment door. (When I had the film processed, the shot was acceptable. Just.)

But the suite was empty. Finnen was furious. The rat had given him the right address but the wrong suite number. Presumably, the bad guy was supposed to hear the racket and get out of Dodge. Somehow (I never found out how), Finnen soon came up with the appropriate suite number. I hopped in an unmarked car with Constable Mark Zenko for a midnight run out to the judge's home at Sproat Lake to amend the warrant.

Back at China Creek Apartments, Finnen tracked down the building manager and talked him into handing over the key to the suspect's suite. This time, he took the lead at the doorway. First, he quietly unlocked the door, listened for a few moments, then slammed on it a couple of times with his fist. With his left hand, he quietly turned the door handle to the open position and held it there.

After a pause, a sleepy but irritated voice said, "Who is it?"

"Police! Open Up!"

Pause.

"Fuck off!"

I hit the shutter again as Finnen shoved the door open, snaked his right hand through the opening, and grabbed the suspect by the throat. This time, my little camera caught only a blur. After the suspect was led away, I joined the detectives who were checking out the heaps of stolen property lying around the suite. I had already taken a few photos when Finnen pulled me aside.

"I have to tell you, you're not really supposed to be in here," he said, and I got one of those sinking feelings. As he explained, a recent decision in the BC Court of Appeal, on what he then believed to be a grow-op takedown, had overturned a conviction because police had allowed a TV film crew to enter the premises and film the bust. (Much later, I learned the case actually involved child pornography, not marijuana.) It was the first I had heard of *R. v. West*, and over the next few years it would drastically affect relations between Canadian police and the media.

According to the appeal document, a journalist with CBC Television had obtained information that the accused, a Mr. West, was engaged in the "production, distribution or possession of pornographic material involving children." After providing police with sufficient evidence to obtain a search warrant, the journalist was invited to accompany police on the takedown. West had asked the CBC team to leave his residence, which they did. However, once the suspect was taken away, they were allowed to shoot the crime scene from the doorway.

At trial, the matter of media presence at the crime scene was the subject of a *voir dire* hearing. The trial judge ruled that all evidence seized at the scene was admissible. Once the evidence was declared admissible, West pleaded guilty to three counts related to child pornography, while at the same time reserving his right to appeal against the ruling of the *voir dire*.

The appeal came before Justices McEachern, Lambert, and Southin on November 5, and on December 10, 1997, they overturned the conviction and ordered a new trial. The search was declared unreasonable under Section 8 of the Canadian Charter of Rights and Freedoms. Of special concern to the three justices was the fact that police had allowed the TV crew to re-enter the scene after West had expressly demanded they vacate the premises.

One year following that appeal, on December 7, 1998, the Monday after the China Creek raid, I published a limited account of it, omitting my entry into the apartment. The main focus of the article was the arrest of the two break-and-enter suspects that had taken place earlier that day, one of whom was Roderick Patten, who was then twenty years old. It was the first time that I'd heard that name. On the same day, the *Times* published a follow-up story from reporter Brian Wilford in which Dan Smith advised that the RCMP were keeping the Carolyn Lee file open. Smith reminded readers that, according to one witness account, there was still a suspect at large: the blond-haired man Alice Lazorko belatedly reported to investigators.

But *R. v. West* would rear its head, with career-threatening potential. Summoned to the RCMP detachment, I found myself confronted by the new police chief, Inspector Lou Racz, and the GIS head, Sergeant John Van Schaik, who had succeeded Dale Djos the previous summer.

It went something like this: "We need to know: did you enter the suite at China Creek Apartments on Friday night?"

Silently cursing Dave Finnen, I denied setting a foot in the suite, despite the existence of a full set of negatives of the search and the stolen property.

"If you entered the suite, it would invalidate the arrest, you know."

Somehow, I suspected Finnen had deliberately used me to queer the bust. At stake was my security clearance, which, due to my position on the local Crime Stoppers executive, was about as high as a civilian could attain. I continued to deny any wrongdoing.

"Shayne, Finnen told us he took you inside. We just need to hear it from you, on the record."

"Well, if Finnen already told you, why the hell do you need to hear it from me?" I said in exasperation, then stopped short. I had walked right into it. They were gracious about it, and my security clearance was not affected. As it turned out, the China Creek Apartments suspect himself was never charged, but he subsequently rolled over on his suppliers, probably never suspecting that my presence at his arrest had conferred immunity on him.

On February 3, Roderick Patten, however, was sentenced to fifteen months in jail on break-and-enter charges.

THE YEAR 1998 marked the passing of a law that would further the evolution of the use of DNA evidence, an evolution critical to the successful prosecution of Patten. The DNA Identification Act had been reborn as Bill C-3 and received its First Reading on September 25, 1997, just three days after the 36th Parliament began sitting. The Second Reading followed on May 12, 1998, and the bill was eventually passed in the House on September 29. On December 8, just five days after Gurmit Singh Dhillon was convicted of first-degree murder, based in part on DNA evidence, senators received the Standing Committee report on the DNA Identification Act. The bill received Third Reading and Royal Assent the following day.

The new legislation allowed the creation of the National DNA Data Bank, which was split into two components. A crime scene index would store DNA profiles derived from genetic materials collected at the scene of a crime in which a designated offence took place, while the convicted offenders index would contain DNA profiles of those convicted of designated offences. The DNA profiles could be created from genetic samples collected voluntarily or under DNA warrant.

Further clauses set out the terms under which genetic material could be preserved and stored, and also set out penalties for anyone convicted of misusing the stored data. The law was made retroactive to allow the sampling of offenders who committed crimes before Bill C-3 came into force. Finally, Clause 22 ensured that DNA information in electronic form would be removed from the data bank "if they established no connection with the crime, the person was finally acquitted, or a year had expired following discharge, stay, dismissal, or withdrawal of charges."

COLD HIT

Eight months after the conviction of Gurmit Dhillon, the RCMP crime lab in Vancouver got the long-awaited cold hit on Sample 700-something —Roderick Patten. The third generation of DNA technology enabled Hiron Poon to make the conclusive nine-loci (plus sex typing) DNA match.

Stefano Mazzega said that, while it makes for good screen drama, forensic lab technicians do not typically shout cheers and slap high-fives when a positive DNA match is confirmed. But this case was different. "Normally, you could be working on up to twenty cases at once. It gets pretty overwhelming, so normally, once the report goes out the door, you move on to something else." Mazzega said that, typically, when the technician had a potential match in hand, there was an extensive quality control procedure to be followed, and "that would be the point where you'd say, 'This is looking good.'" At this point, the scientist said, a recording officer would likely advise his colleagues that a potential match was at hand. He might give the lead investigator a heads-up that one of his suspects was a likely match in order to focus the team resources more effectively.

Mazzega said that the States case had generated so many samples that were systematically eliminated that there could have been a tendency for the analysts to become blasé about the investigation. But something was different about June 23, 1999. Hiron Poon says he remembers the moment vividly. On that day, there was a meeting scheduled with his supervisor and members of the lab crew, including Mazzega. He had a load of work to review, but for some reason, he had a feeling that something was about to break. He decided to risk a breach of protocol and asked to be excused from the meeting.

"At the time, I was busy analyzing the data. By then, after two years, I pretty well had the [suspect] profile memorized in my head. So when the DNA profile came up, I saw it right away. I recognized it. I went over to the meeting room and said, 'Hey—I've got a match!' I also called Dan [Smith's] office." Within an hour, the news had spread throughout the lab.

Poon had been looking for Dan Smith at the GIS office, but it was Shelley Arnfield who took the call. "Dan had just gone on holiday when Hiron phoned, and he said to me 'Are you sitting down? We've got a match.' And I immediately just grabbed my big black binder, and I said, 'What number, Hiron?'"

When she checked the "700-something" number in her binder, she was shocked. "Roddy Patten. I thought, 'I've known that kid since 1991.' I had expected it to be 'somebody you didn't know.' But ... I had known this kid for all that time. He was twelve when I arrived [in Port Alberni], and I had been dealing with him for years." Arnfield said the revelation brought a full mix of emotions in addition to simple stunned shock that the suspect had been in plain sight the whole time. "I sat there and thought, besides the guys in the lab, I am the only person in the world who knows who did it."

That day, only Arnfield and fellow GIS member Steve Sawlewicz were on duty. "I said to Steve, 'They've got a match.' And Steve said, 'Okay! We've got to write the DNA warrant!'"

Here, she paused. "Neither of us has a clue how to write a DNA warrant, and Dan has gone on holidays. He's off fishing in the toolies somewhere. So [Constable] Terry Horrocks came on at four o'clock for the night shift. I said, 'Terry, we've got a hit. We've got to find Dan.' Terry took charge because he knew the general area where Dan had gone fishing. He got the Forest Rangers to go out in the bush, find Dan, and get him to call Terry."

Smith said he had barely settled in at his campsite when Arnfield received the news from Poon. "I had taken some annual leave. Because of these files, I was perpetually behind in my annual leave." Smith had set up a campsite at the Ralph River Campground on Buttle Lake in the Campbell River area. According to the plan, his family would join him in a few days. He paid his camp fees and had just cooked a hamburger on his portable barbecue.

"I was relaxing when the camp ranger drove up and stopped at my campsite. I'm thinking he wanted to collect the camp fees, which I have already paid. I was trying to explain to him that I'd already paid the fees at the Ranger Station. He said, 'It's nothing about that. Are you Mr. Smith? Are you a member of the RCMP?'"

When Smith confirmed his identity, the ranger advised that he had an important message. "I can't remember the exact message, but he said, 'There's been a hit,' or 'There's been a development in one of your files. You need to get back to Port Alberni right away.'"

While Smith had a number of active files in process, he knew there was only one case that would move his colleagues to tear him away from a long-needed vacation. Smith said he doesn't even remember if he folded up his tent properly. "I threw everything in my truck and roared back and got the news," he said. "We delved into it. That was better than any vacation. Shortly after I got called back, I spoke to Hiron Poon. He told me about the match with the consent sample. And he said, at that time, the odds were 1.9 trillion to one. That's eleven zeros after the 1.9." Legally speaking, odds of over a thousand to one is considered "very strong evidence," Smith explained. "This is 1.9 trillion to one. That's 'unbelievably strong evidence.'" But there was still a lengthy process that analysts and detectives had to undertake before Roderick Patten could be arrested and charged with murder.

NOW, WITH THE suspect identified, strategy became critical. Before he transferred out to the Campbell River detachment a year earlier, in July 1998, Dale Djos had put an operational plan in place to be followed when a killer was identified. Smith had officially taken over as lead investigator in the Jessica States case, but he fully expected to roll out the operational plan as laid down by Djos.

The plan was a modified version of the Mr. Big Sting that has since fallen into disrepute because of the number of false convictions the tactic has produced. Briefly, it works like this: Undercover officers "befriend" a suspect, in some instances paying him to perform certain tasks, not always illegal. Once the suspect is drawn in, he meets the mysterious Mr. Big, who is yet another undercover officer. Mr. Big demands that the suspect reveal his criminal credentials in detail if he is going to be elevated to a higher, more lucrative role in the "organization." Mr. Big wants to know, "What's the worst thing you've ever done?"

Ideally, the suspect confesses to the specific crime that police are investigating. Prodded for more information, he provides details that would be known only to the perpetrator and the investigators can build a bulletproof case against him. The "confession" is but one part of an unshakeable chain of evidence leading to a conviction. The confession itself becomes the single most important piece of evidence against them and is sufficient to bring about a conviction. Justice is done. But faced with a one-time opportunity to make easy money with a certain amount of protection, suspects subjected to the Mr. Big scenario are easily swayed to make detailed confessions to crimes they did not commit.

In this case, Smith already had the DNA evidence indisputably linking Roderick Patten to the crime scene. Or at least, he had the proof of guilt. But only if he could put it before a court of law. "By this time we had a lot of experience dealing with DNA evidence," Smith said. "We had already lost one consent sample in the Dhillon case. If the consent sample does not go in—if the suspect says 'somebody threatened me to get the sample,' we've got nothing."

In the modified Mr. Big scenario, investigators would attempt to obtain a confession as grounds for a DNA warrant while collecting cast-off DNA from their suspect. "At the time the cold hit came up, Patten was already in jail on the B & E charges, and he wasn't due for release for months, so we had all the time we needed to set it up."

There was a second prong in the campaign to obtain a DNA warrant for Patten, and it was based on a fundamental eccentricity within the Charter of Rights and Freedoms. The Charter will protect you from unreasonable search and seizure of DNA if you are an accused criminal. But it has nothing to say if you are not accused of any crime. Smith said he could not take credit for the tactic that subsequently secured the DNA warrant. In a reprise of the reconstruction of Carolyn Lee's DNA profile through the profiling of her parents, when the crime lab reported the cold hit on Roderick Patten, Smith and his team launched a DNA collection on Patten's parents, Alma and Roderick Patten Sr. On July 25, just two days after the cold hit, a female officer from Courtenay collected a cast-off DNA sample from Rod Sr.

"We had previously obtained a birth certificate for Roddy Patten from the provincial government. From there, we found both his parents living in Port Alberni. That was through the police database. The father lived in a trailer that was for sale. We had [the undercover officer] meet him to look at the trailer. Then she took him out for coffee over at the Barclay Hotel. While they're there, he's smoking and drinking coffee. We took the cigarette butts and the coffee cup and extracted his DNA."

The next day, Arnfield and Smith met with Patten's mother and sister, Alma and Michelle. In the years after the trial, rumours swirled around suggesting that Alma Patten had known about the killing and shielded her son from police, but both Dan Smith and Dale Djos have categorically rejected the idea that Alma had any knowledge of the crime. At the time of the cold hit, Alma Patten and her daughter, Michelle, lived in the South Port area, next door to a known female drug dealer who was under police surveillance. This was fortuitous because Smith had a legitimate reason to arrange an interview with the two women—to learn more about activities around the drug house next door to them.

Smith could not just drop by the Patten house, even in plain-clothes and driving an unmarked police cruiser. A visit from police could conceivably put the mother and daughter in jeopardy from their neighbour and her associates. Smith and Arnfield arranged to meet the Pattens at Tim Hortons, located well on the other side of town.

During the conversation, Alma Patten momentarily threw the two investigators into a quiet panic when she mentioned that "she had thirteen foster children. Our hearts just sank at that moment because we're thinking, 'Oh no—is [Roddy] one of the foster children, and was this not on the birth certificate?' But then, she talked about her three [biological] children—Michelle, Jennifer, and Roddy Patten."

"At that point, Roddy was in jail on B & E charges," said Smith, "and [Alma] felt terrible about that. I felt bad for her that we were putting her in this spot [when] she alluded to how she still had hope for him, that he could still turn his life around. But the essential element was that she explained that 'her only son who she gave birth to' was Roddy. So we were okay. And we also knew there were no brothers we were dealing with. After they left ... we put on gloves, and then bagged up their cups."

Smith sent the samples to Hiron Poon at the forensic lab in Vancouver. "I gave them a table of statistics saying that, from the DNA obtained at the crime scene, this is the probability that it came from the offspring of the ... family," Poon said. Poon was asked if, had it later been proven that Rod Sr. was not the genetic father of Rod Jr., could the composite family profile have excluded the suspect? "If [Rod] Sr. was not the dad, we would have been able to tell right away," he explained. "In this particular case, everything did match up." Had it not, Poon said having the linkage through the mother was more critical. "The number would not be as good as having both of the parents. But in this case, everything worked out well. So we could say that, 'Yes. There is a very high probability that the person who left the biological sample at the crime scene is the offspring of these parents.' With that, you can get a warrant."

And for Smith, obtaining that warrant was the priority. "We got our match. He established odds of 14.9 million to one that the male DNA from the chewing gum was from a biological child of Alma and Roderick Patten Sr. That's for the Caucasian population. It increases to 333 million to one for the Coastal Salish population. Patten has some Salish ancestry." The findings would subsequently provide "reasonable and probable grounds" for a DNA warrant.

"On a warrant, you're looking for 'reasonable and probable grounds,' not 'beyond a reasonable doubt,' so this was a very high standard. Based on that, we went ahead to get the DNA warrant." Smith said the original consent sample had been collected when Patten and his associates came under suspicion. However, should the consent sample have been tossed out, that would have broken the chain to the DNA warrant, had the DNA sampling of Alma and Rod Patten Sr. not been conducted. By definition, that sampling was not a "search," and therefore, no one's Charter rights were being violated. A citizen does not have a Charter standing in a case in which they are not a suspect, he explained.

Arnfield said that by now, she and her colleagues had become quite adept at collecting cast-off samples. "Terry [Horrocks] wasn't even working one day ... when he sees the guy that we know we need a sample from. He followed the guy into Tim Hortons and grabbed a spoon." Another potential suspect was sampled at a Tim Hortons in Courtenay. "He was having coffee and he wiped his nose with a napkin and left it on a tray. When they left, Dan and I sat down in their seats, put on the gloves, and packed it up." A sample collected discreetly like this allowed the investigators, under the Charter of Rights, a to build a DNA profile that would hold up in court when Jessica's killer finally came to trial.

While Smith may have intended to pursue a careful, measured strategy as the three-year anniversary of Jessica States's murder approached, a double homicide threw local investigators into a frenzy during the final week of July 1999.

On the night of Sunday, July 25, in an apparent drug rip-off, two suspects entered an apartment building in the Glenwood neighbourhood at about 10:30. One male victim was beaten over the head with a claw hammer before being shot, while a second man was also shot.

Monday night was a regularly scheduled city council meeting, so I worked a split shift that day. Despite my good working relations with local RCMP, they weren't revealing much that morning about the assaults on Sunday evening. By deadline I had found out independently that a firearm had been used, but no one at the detachment would confirm it. The names of the victims had not been released, but that was pretty standard. I wrote a short summary of the "serious assault" with the information provided by the RCMP, and a roundup of events from the weekend, before heading home at lunchtime.

On a normal council night, I would have headed to city hall and compiled enough material to keep me going for a few days. I would intersperse infrastructure expenditures, zoning amendments, and water main repairs amid the tire slashings, kitchen fires, and prize pumpkins of small-town life. But some time just before five that afternoon, my publisher called me at home. He had heard something on the police scanner. All he knew was that every available police and ambulance unit had just converged on the 3000 block of First Avenue, less than ten blocks from where I lived. I grabbed my camera bag and was there in minutes. I parked outside the police tape cordon and loaded a fresh roll of colour film into my camera.

After three years on the job, I had been to plenty of crime scenes and knew what to expect. I approached the police cordon at a steady pace with the Nikon at waist level, set at wide angle. When I came close to the scene, I started snapping frames, swinging from left to right, fully expecting to catch the sequence where the cop barges in, waving his arms and telling me "no pictures."

It didn't happen. With half a roll left, I snapped a few shots of the emergency vehicles parked in front of a small wood frame house on the east side of the street. I zoomed in on a couple sitting on the curb: a young woman, obviously distraught, and a young man, obviously her partner, comforting her. I soon learned there were two dead bodies in the home and that the young woman, who lived in the home, had discovered the crime scene. There was already suspicion that the shooting was related to the incident of the previous night.

By now, both the Vancouver and the Island District Serious Crimes units had arrived on the scene, which would make getting official information a little more difficult. What I knew by deadline: the victims were a young man and a young woman. The distraught young woman I'd take a photo of was the sister of the dead woman, and police confirmed that she was a resident of the home. She was taken to the RCMP detachment to make a statement and to receive counselling from the Victim Services Program. Neither the names of the victims nor the manner of death had been released, and autopsies were to be performed later in the day. Police now reported that one of the victims in the Sunday night shooting had been airlifted to Victoria in serious condition and investigators were trying to determine whether the two crimes were related.

The next morning, after I wrapped up and sent my copy to the editor, I got a whispered call from the front desk. The parents of the murdered woman were in the office to put together an obituary. I asked the editor to hold the front page in the event I could pick up something useful.

Their names were Don and Lillian Campbell, and from what they told me, I was able to put together a detailed story. Their murdered daughter, Lorinda, was twenty years old, and her deceased partner was Michael Walker. The girl on the curb had been Lorinda's eighteen-year-old younger sister, Angel, and her boyfriend, Brent LaFlamme. LaFlamme owned the home where the couple was killed. Don and Lillian owned the home directly across the street. They were out of town at the time of the shooting. "We had to go to the morgue this morning to identify our daughter," Don Campbell told me. He also confirmed how the two were killed. "She was shot. I saw her."

Campbell acknowledged that there was drug activity in the LaFlamme house and police were having a difficult time with potential witnesses. "They say they're not getting very much cooperation," he said. "It seems that some people don't want to mention things for fear of implicating themselves in other crimes ... This is a murder—that's our daughter lying there in the morgue. Everybody loved Lorinda. If they were her friends, they should come forward. That would be the best way they could pay their respects, to tell police everything they know." For the waiting editor, I packaged their call for cooperation with a photo of the distraught parents taken on the spot.

On Wednesday, July 28, police revealed that Walker and Campbell were both shot in the head, "execution-style." I learned that Walker was known as a very tough guy who collected drug debts for local dealers. Once I had finished for the day, I headed over to the Campbell residence. Campbell was frankly worried for his surviving daughter's safety, and there had been speculation that police had spirited Angel and Brent out of town for their own protection. Don's public appeal, however, had inspired otherwise reluctant people to come forward with information.

On Tuesday, August 3, an RCMP team led by Dan Smith apprehended Allan Larry Thomas, a close acquaintance of Walker and the Campbells, and charged him with two counts of first-degree murder. That morning, Susan Roth, who occasionally did freelance photography for the *Times*, was at the home of a friend who lived across the street from Thomas. When police vehicles suddenly appeared in front of the house across the street, she quickly pulled out her camera and shot a sequence of photos as the Emergency Response Team members smashed through the front door of the Thomas house.

But even more devastating for the Campbells was the arrest of Brent LaFlamme on charges of robbery and using a firearm in the course of a robbery, in connection with the July 25 shootings. As it transpired, LaFlamme not only took part in the Sunday night robbery, but he was also on hand early the next morning when Thomas gunned down Campbell and Walker. After the killings, the two walked to a nearby bar and had several drinks. They later drifted up to Walker's home, where they drank the last beers in the refrigerator and made several long-distance phone calls. When the bodies hadn't been discovered by late afternoon the next day, LaFlamme sent Angel into the house, knowing she would be met with a scene of utter horror.

Once again, within days Port Alberni RCMP had captured a killer whose crimes shocked the city. The case served as a reminder that there was still a child murderer out there, and an entire community was waiting for him to be brought to justice.

"DON'T LOOK FOR A MONSTER"

On July 31, the three-year anniversary of the Jessica States murder, Dan Smith spoke with Louise Dickson, a reporter for the Victoria *Times Colonist*, expressing his confidence that Jessica's killer would be caught "because police discovered a DNA sample left behind by the killer." Smith noted that investigators had taken four hundred DNA samples from people in Port Alberni and the Indigenous community of Ahousaht. "Police have even gone so far as to take DNA samples from people who have died suddenly, in case death would conceal the killer's identity," the article continued.

Dickson also contacted Dale Djos at the RCMP detachment in Campbell River. Despite transferring up-Island with a promotion the previous year, Djos was still emotionally invested in the case. She also noted that "the investigation was delayed this week by a shooting and double slaying believed to be drug-related." Smith said, "I want the community to bear with us. We will catch this person and they can rest easy that we will."

With a killer on the loose in those last days of July and a full-blown homicide investigation taking up much of my time the previous week, I hadn't written anything to mark the three-year anniversary of the Jessica States murder. But when I finally sat down with Dan Smith, I didn't know that he already had the killer's identity established, and in hindsight, I appreciate the legal tightrope he was walking while waiting to establish grounds for a warranted DNA sample.

My contribution to the article, co-written with reporter Karen Beck, began with a nod to the genetic manhunt being conducted in science labs across North America. This was Dan Smith's opening gambit both in preparing the suspect for future interrogation and to encourage potential witnesses to recall any involvement they may have had with him, criminal or otherwise: "At this stage, investigators say they are looking for the usual suspect in long-standing murder investigations: the one 'nobody ever would have suspected,'" I wrote.

"'Don't look for a monster,' said investigation coordinator Cpl. Dan Smith. 'It's normal to expect that someone who does something terrible will look the part. But most often, somebody who does something terrible goes back to looking and acting normal again.'"

Smith told me that after years of conducting successful interrogations, the "no monster" approach was his most frequently used technique. "The one I preferred allows a person to confess to a crime and still save some face. In other words, nobody is going to yell at them that they are a child-killer who sexually molests children. But they might confess to doing that in a way that makes it understandable to a greater number of people."

Smith had fully intended to follow the strategy laid down by Dale Djos in the event the killer was identified by a cold DNA hit. But inexplicably, especially in light of the double homicide investigation still underway, Smith's RCMP commanders decided to toss that strategy out the window.

Smith said he made his objections to the change in strategy clear. If Patten were able to invalidate the consent sample taken in September 1997, the entire chain of evidence would fall apart. Recalling the events when talking with me fifteen years later, the tension was still palpable. "I am directed to go to the jail where he is being held, in the Fraser Valley, and arrest him for the murder. I did not want to do it. I had to be ordered to do it," he said tersely. "I was of the view that we should stick with the original operational plan, which would almost certainly yield the results that we wanted, based on our past understanding of the law." But Smith, accompanied by an RCMP constable from the Courtenay detachment, apprised Patten of the case against him and made the arrest. Patten was transported to the Maple Ridge RCMP detachment for the initial interview where he was represented (by telephone) by Port Alberni lawyer John Bennie.

Smith said that Patten refused to make a statement, but in the course of the initial visit, he did say something that suggested he'd been thinking about a possible legal defence. "He said something like, 'Oh man. I'm going to get twenty-five years to life for something that I didn't do the worst part of,' implying that someone else did the crime and he'd just left his DNA there."

Patten was flown to Port Alberni by helicopter, where he engaged local defence counsel Charles Beckingham to represent him. Once again, he refused to cooperate with the RCMP. That left Smith with DNA from a consent sample as the only tangible evidence of Patten's guilt. He felt he needed to build a much more substantial case against him just in case the sample was thrown out of court. More specifically, he wanted to establish grounds for a warranted DNA sample that did not flow from the cold hit. But on paper, the Mounties had their man and they weren't about to keep it quiet, especially after three years of frustration and a thousand DNA samples. They chose the morning of Tuesday, August 10, 1999, to make the announcement.

ARREST OVERSHADOWS HEROISM

As the result of unusually large snow packs from the previous winter, water levels in the Somass River had been much higher and temperatures much colder than usual throughout the late spring and summer. And this led to a tragedy that would be sadly overshadowed by the momentous news about the States case.

Just after dinner on August 9, I received a call at home from one of the *Times* mailroom crew who lived on the river near the Riverbend (Orange) Bridge. Police and Alberni Valley Rescue personnel were gathered on the beach near the foot of the bridge, and I was told to check it out.

Corporal Dave Finnen, now serving as watch commander, filled me in. A sixteen-year-old girl, later identified as Alisha Smith, had been swimming at Papermill Dam, just upriver from the bridge, with her six-year-old brother and a girlfriend. When her little brother slipped out of his float tube, Alisha, an outstanding athlete, swam out into the fast-flowing water and pulled him to shore. But just as she pushed him into waiting hands on shore, her clothing became entangled in a mass of floating log debris, and she was dragged to her death.

The next morning, I wrote about the drowning with an emphasis on safety. I quoted Finnen extensively on the dangers posed by the unseasonably high waters and treacherously unpredictable currents. The story was set for the top of the front page. Then, just before eleven, I got a phone call from Sergeant John Van Schaik, asking me to come over to his office.

"We've got something to share with you. It should only take about fifteen minutes." I made some calculations. Five minutes to the RCMP detachment to find out what they wanted. The editor has to send page one in by 11:30 that morning. My story was wrapped. Anything I picked up now would run tomorrow, unless it was very short and red-hot. At the RCMP detachment, the receptionist buzzed me in. "They're in John's office. They're waiting for you," she said. I knew the way to the GIS office.

The police chief, Lou Racz, was seated next to John Van Schaik, the head of the GIS. Both wore an expression similar to the one they'd had when they admonished me about entering the scene of the China Creek Apartment bust. *What the hell did I do this time?* I thought.

"It's Jessica ..." said Van Schaik.

MY HEAD WAS still spinning as Racz and Van Schaik filled me in on the details. The suspect was twenty years old and had been charged with first-degree murder but could not be named yet because he was a young offender at the time of the crime. The Crown would apply to have him elevated to adult court. He was currently in custody on unrelated charges.

I made the short drive back to the *Times* office, trying to figure out how we could get this news story on the front page, which might already be on the press. I stumbled past the reception desk and down the hall into the newsroom. The editor was just about to send the last page. All eyes looked up as I stood in the doorway and croaked: "Hold page one!" That set off a storm of indignation, as expected. As the initial wave of "What the fuck?" died down, I said the magic two words: "It's Jessica ..."

All arguments ceased. The editor cleared the bottom of the front page and moved the tragic drowning down-page. (All these years later, I still feel a pang of regret that this heroic young girl's sacrifice went "below the fold.") I had a red-hot story to write, and Racz had advised that he wasn't going to issue a media release until we went to press, so I banged out a report in the accepted Canadian Press style: a one-sentence lede announcing the arrest, one three-sentence paragraph outlining the suspect, the charges, and his young offender status, and a quote to begin the third paragraph:

"We've known his identity for about a month and a half, but it's taken a lot of determined police work to provide confirmation," Van Schaik advised. I recounted the bare facts of the crime and the principal investigators and cited Dan Smith's thoughts from the previous week. It was just over four hundred words and ran with the now familiar school photo of Jessica. We were already well past deadline by the time I finished, and the press crew was waiting for the plates, but this was one of those days where there was no question about dishing out overtime. I had one more person to quote, though.

As lead investigator in the Jessica States investigation, Dale Djos had driven himself to the limit. Even after transferring to Campbell River, he had maintained close contact with investigators on the case, and with Jessica's parents. Fortunately, I was able to catch him at his desk, and we spoke briefly. "It was unfinished business," said Djos. "I still have Jessica's picture on my desk blotter as a constant reminder. We had a tour come through here, and one of the visitors asked who the little girl was. I guess it's more common to have pictures of your own kids on your desk."

Rob and Dianne States had been located at their campsite on nearby Great Central Lake and informed of the arrest. Later that day, the *Times* received a handwritten press release from the States family:

> At this present time we're all feeling overwhelmed and have many mixed emotions. We do want to express our appreciation to the police for their compassion, kindness, understanding & most of all their hard work & dedication. We are also thankful to our friends, family, media & to the community with a heart for their kindness & support.
>
> We are hopeful that justice will prevail. Please remember Jessica for who she was—her bubbling personality and her outgoing nature. Regardless, nothing is going to bring Jessica back, but perhaps now she can rest in peace.

Speaking to the Victoria *Times Colonist*, Dianne States expressed her relief. Rob called it the light at the end of the tunnel. "It's been hard on the three of us," Rob said. "If anything, it has brought us closer together, not torn us apart." Regarding the suspect, Rob expressed disgust. "For starters, the fact that he is a man makes me ashamed to be one." Jessica's grandfather, eighty-year-old Bob States, was asked what he would say to the suspect: "If I could, I wouldn't say anything to him. I'd just wring his neck."

ON AUGUST 11, Patten made his first appearance at a court in Port Alberni. The States family and their supporters were seated in one front row, accompanied by an armed and uniformed police officer. Also seated in the gallery were John Van Schaik and Dan Smith, both in plainclothes.

In the opposite front row, a full contingent of *Alberni Valley Times* reporters and out-of-town media members waited for their first look at the suspect. Security was tight. Allan Larry Thomas, the suspect in the recent double homicide, was scheduled to make an appearance in the afternoon session, along with a twelve-year-old charged with arson. Ten additional sheriff's deputies checked bags, and anyone entering Courtroom 2 had to pass through a metal detector.

The mood was tense. One well-known Vancouver reporter who had written extensively on the investigation attempted to take a seat on the front bench. "Reserved for media," one of my burly young *Times* colleagues snarled at him.

"What do you think I am?" the interloper asked.

"I don't know who the fuck you are," my colleague growled. The Vancouver reporter took a seat in the second row.

At eleven o'clock, following the morning recess, Roddy Patten was led into the prisoner's dock by an armed sheriff. Carol Lazar, the presiding judge, read the charge for which Port Alberni residents had been waiting for more than three years: "You are charged with the first-degree murder of Jessica Dianne States under Section 235 of the Canadian Criminal Code."

Patten slumped visibly in the dock as Lazar read the charge against him. Charles Beckingham, his defence counsel, immediately asked for a publication ban on evidence released during the hearing as well as a six-week adjournment. Lazar questioned the need for the publication ban, as neither side was presenting prejudicial evidence during the brief court appearance, but she did grant the six-week adjournment.

The judge then directed her remarks to the accused in the dock. "This matter will proceed in adult court unless you make application to the Attorney General's Office to be heard in youth court," she advised. Speculation was that the accused would have little chance of having his case heard in youth court.

Following the court appearance, the States family members were escorted out of the building. Rob States later told the *Times Colonist* that he "came close" to bolting over the bar and into the prisoner's dock, but he was able to restrain himself. Asked what he was thinking during the appearance, he replied, "The first thing that came to my mind was to piss on his grave."

For his first court appearance, Patten was conducted back and forth to the courthouse in a police car, rather than in the sheriff's van. In part, that was to maintain continuity with the suspect, Smith explained. Had Patten decided to make a confession out of the presence of the police, it may have created some legal difficulties about its admissibility as evidence.

THE CONFESSION

Now Smith was able to collect the all-important warranted DNA sample. "At this point, we've all been taking DNA samples for a long time, and I was confident that we would be deemed capable of doing that within the legal parameters of the Criminal Code. But nonetheless, to be ultra-sure—because I'm getting a little spooked now about the consent sample—I found a member, [Constable] Shelley Birston, who was also a registered nurse ... She said she had taken over four thousand blood samples without difficulty. In a warrant, you have to name the person who is going to take the blood samples, and they have to be, by virtue of training and experience, doing it safely." With this overabundance of caution, Smith and Birston collected the sample at the Port Alberni cellblock.

Smith walked into the interview room with his "no monster" opening strategy, and it paid off immediately. The confession, when it came, was abject, and it was detailed.

"We had been working eighteen-hour days. We were kind of burned out and frazzled. I thought it worthwhile to give him one last effort to confess." Smith said he conducted Patten from the cellblock to the interview room in the GIS office. "This is very fresh in my mind because this is a highlight in my career. It really stands out," he said. "I had arranged to have [police] standing at each of the three doorways in which a person could exit our building, between the cellblock and the interview room, just to prevent any chance to escape."

The first step, he explained, was to set up a positive confrontation. "Part of that positive confrontation is letting him know that I know—there is no one else involved. Just him." That was calculated to shut down the avenue Patten had tried to open with his spontaneous statement that "I didn't even do the worst part."

"I had the stack of files sitting there. I wanted him to know that we had investigated all of the people he associated with and that he implied were involved in the murder." When Smith made his first approach, Patten did not have counsel in the room, so any comments or admissions the suspect made would be subject to legal examination. That tactic gives the interviewee a slight margin of error in the event of any unplanned utterances.

"I said, 'You know, everybody in Port Alberni thinks that the person who did this is a monster—someone who lies in wait for little children so they can rape and murder them. I don't think that's what happened. I think that this was a momentary loss of control. Five minutes before this, you wouldn't have done it; five minutes after this, you wouldn't have done it. For that very short period of time, you lost control and you did something you regret. If I'm right, I'd like to hear that from you. But if I'm wrong—if you are that kind of person—if you are that monster lying in wait for little children, then maybe the best thing to do is say nothing.'"

At that point, Patten must have realized the weight of evidence against him. But with years of experience before the courts, both as a young offender and as an adult, Patten also knew how the system worked. "I want to tell you what happened," he told Smith, "but I want my lawyer present." Smith called a break while he contacted Charles Beckingham's office. The lawyer arrived and was apprised of his client's intention to confess.

From Patten's description of the chain of events leading to Jessica States's death, it was heartbreakingly obvious that the very qualities that made the eleven-year-old so unique—her fearlessness, her fierce sense of independence, and even her boyish appearance—had placed her in harm's way. According to Patten, when Jessica encountered the burly young man in the woods adjacent to the ballpark, she didn't run away. "He confessed to, at first, thinking that Jessica was a boy, and said, 'How's it going, little man?'" Rather than letting a chance comment from a complete stranger simply pass, Jessica apparently felt a need to let him know who he was dealing with. It was a tragic mis-calculation. "She said, 'I'm not a man. I'm a girl,' and showed him the waistband on her panties."

Patten confessed that this simple revelation of prepubescent femi-nine underwear was enough to trigger a savage rape response. Patten immediately punched the girl on the head, which was likely the cause of significant brain stem injuries, as later corroborated by the coro-ner's report. In the course of the interview, he told interrogators that he was a pretty fearsome fighter and that, even as a teenager, he had knocked out grown men with a single punch. "He decided he wanted to have sex with her, so he punched her. He didn't give her a chance to say no. He had sex with her. And when she wouldn't stop moving, he killed her," Smith said.

Smith explained that, according to the medical examiner, the injured girl was likely unconscious and undergoing convulsions as a result of the initial blow to the head. "That squares with the autopsy results—because of damage to the upper central nervous system," he said.

Smith said while there was no "silver lining," he was later able to comfort Jessica's parents, somewhat, by telling them their daugh-ter was almost certainly unconscious from the first moments of the assault. That information, however, was classified as "holdback" evi-dence, and was not made public, even to the family, until the trial finally went to court. At this point, however, the facts of the matter were incontestable.

"He admitted killing her. He admitted *most* of the damage that he did. He admitted having sex with her." Smith said despite being ensconced in the interview room, there was one outside interruption recorded on the interview videotape. "He was sobbing during the interview. At one point, right at the critical moment, a motorcycle drives by the detachment and it sort of drowns out what he's trying to say. You can hear through it, but it makes it more difficult—which is unfortunate."

Smith said he gave Patten every opportunity to offer any miti-gating circumstances. "At the conclusion, I asked him of there was anything important that we hadn't talked about. And he said no."

Smith said the significance of this was that, at trial nearly two years later, Patten would provide an elaborate story of ripping off an outdoor marijuana grow-op to purchase a large quantity of LSD, which subsequently rendered him legally incapable of forming criminal intent. The drug-defence testimony would later generate major headlines. But police had already established that, at the time of the confession, Patten made no effort to explain his behaviour.

ON SEPTEMBER 22, 1999, Patten made his second appearance in court, again under heavy security, to set a date for a preliminary hearing and to hear an application from defence counsel that the matter be held in provincial youth court. Those who attended were again required to pass through a metal detector at the door. Patten, this time with his hair cropped to the scalp and leg shackles jangling audibly, was led into the dock.

Sid Clark, the presiding judge, immediately ordered a publication ban on evidence revealed at the hearing, then called the case forward in adult court. David Kidd, the same Crown counsel as in the Dhillon trial, was granted a date of March 17, 2000, for a preliminary hearing of the evidence in the case. Kidd estimated he would need four court days to present the Crown's case. Beckingham then made an application under Section 16 (Subsection 1.01) of the Young Offenders Act to have the matter heard in the provincial youth court. Judge Clark simply asked the attending bailiff to call the youth court list, and the proceedings immediately fell under the Young Offenders Act.

Kidd asked the judge to order a predisposition report, and due to the severe nature of the crime, a psychiatric assessment. Beckingham doubled down, requesting a neuropsychological examination to be added to the court assessment. Judge Clark assented to each request. Kidd then advised that this court-ordered assessment could not be completed within the normal thirty-day requirement, and Beckingham agreed to waive it. Kidd anticipated that the psychiatric assessment could be completed by January. Clark then set a date of November 3 to hear the application to try the case in youth court. Kidd, for the record, said the Crown would oppose the application.

Following the hearing, I spoke with Crown counsel Steve Stirling, who explained the different prospects the accused faced if tried in adult court versus youth court. The stakes were significant. If convicted of first-degree murder in adult court, the accused would receive a mandatory sentence of life imprisonment. But because he was only seventeen at the time of the crime, he would be eligible for parole in ten years. If convicted in youth court, he would serve "a period that shall not exceed ten years."

But there was a big "however." That ten-year sentence would consist of a custodial sentence "which shall not exceed six years," followed by four years conditional supervision. In practical terms, "conditional supervision" is the same as parole. That distinction between a young offender and an adult would play out just days before the next hearing.

THE GRIM REAPER AFFAIR

Halloween night of 1999 proved to be yet another lively night for police and police reporter in Port Alberni. I was on a ride-along, and the early part of the evening was largely uneventful. But at 10:30, a sixty-seven-year-old cab driver, Jerry Gill, stumbled up to the front door of a home in the Beaver Creek district. Gill told police he had been robbed by two passengers. One of the suspects was wearing a costume and face makeup—and he was packing a large handgun. Gill vaulted out of the cab and took cover in some nearby shrubbery while the suspects sped off with his cab.

The suspects soon abandoned the cab and began running toward town along the railway tracks near the McLean Mill National Heritage Site. Several kilometres later, they encountered RCMP Constable Eric Sheppard and auxiliary Constable Perry Shepard. Hearing the sound of heavy footfalls in the darkness, the two officers braced for a confrontation. Suddenly, the Grim Reaper burst into the clearing (his accomplice was not costumed). In the darkness, Sheppard and Shepard immediately took the pair to the ground, hearing an audible "clunk" in the process. That clunk proved to be a fully loaded, long-barrel .357 Magnum revolver, recently stolen from the home of a retired police officer.

The two suspects appeared in provincial court on Monday, November 1. The Grim Reaper proved to be a twenty-one-year-old former Port Alberni resident who later pled guilty to one count of using a firearm in the commission of a robbery and one count of using a disguise in the commission of an offence, with a minimum sentence of four years in custody. His accomplice, however, was five days short of his eighteenth birthday, thereby falling under the Young Offenders Act. He would later receive two years' probation.

The next court stop in the States case occurred two days later, when defence lawyer Charles Beckingham appeared before a judge to ask that his client be tried as a young offender. The hearing was set for January 18 to 21, 2000.

Boy Tried as Man

T HE NEW YEAR held a surprise for those following the prosecution of Roddy Patten. On Wednesday, January 5, the court was scheduled to hear an application from defence counsel Charles Beckingham to have his trial moved to the provincial youth court. Instead, the suspect, now twenty-one, asked the judge to dismiss his application, clearing the way for trial in adult court. Judge Brian Klaver ordered the case to proceed directly to preliminary hearing on March 17.

With Patten's identity now out in the open, I interviewed Dan Smith. Headlined "States Investigator Familiar with Long Hunts," the piece I wrote focussed on the link between the Lee and States homicides, with Smith as the fulcrum. The investigator noted that it had taken just over three years to identify Roddy Patten as the suspect in the July 31, 1996, killing, "about a third as long as I put in on the Carolyn Lee investigation," he said. I reminded readers of the timeline of the Lee case, since Smith himself compared the two timelines: "Cpl. Smith doggedly pursued the Carolyn Lee case for nine years after he inherited the file in the mid-1980s. Gurmit Singh Dhillon was convicted of the 1977 murder on Dec. 3, 1998, nearly 21 years after the 12-year-old was killed."

Smith emphasized that investigators had relied heavily on cooperation from the public. Along with those 450-plus voluntary blood samples, police conducted over 3,400 interviews and followed up on over a thousand tips. Police also obtained a number of genetic samples via DNA warrant, he noted.

Two days after Patten was named as the suspect, Jessica's father, Rob States, spoke to the *Times*. He expressed his confidence that police had the right man. "We're glad that he's going to be in adult court. We can see the light at the end of the tunnel now. We're hoping that this will soon be over and we can find some closure. We want to get on with our lives." States conceded that "closure" would never mean that their pain had gone away completely. Whatever life his family might "get on with" would never be the same as it was before July 31, 1996. "Make no mistake—our lives have been devastated by this jerk," he said.

States also said that Patten's decision to withdraw the application to hold the trial in youth court came as a surprise. The family had been prepared to attend the four-day application hearing. Now, their sights were set on the preliminary hearing in March. He conceded that a trial would be traumatic for his family, as they would hear all the evidence surrounding Jessica's violent death. "But we'll be there. I wouldn't miss a minute of it, although I keep hoping he will plead guilty and spare us all the pain."

The prosecutor, David Kidd, explained that an accused in a first-degree murder case could consent to go directly to trial in BC Supreme Court, where he would have the option of pleading guilty or not guilty. But either way, a preliminary hearing was still required in a provincial court. Kidd noted, however, that should the defendant indicate an intention to enter a guilty plea, there would be no need to present evidence at the prelim.

States said police had done a good job keeping the family advised on developments in the case. He summed up with an image that was to recur numerous times as the case proceeded. "Maybe, as a community, we can breathe just a little bit easier now. Our children will never again have the kind of freedom they would like, but now one boogeyman is gone, anyway."

DNA TAKES THE NEXT STEP

The DNA Data Bank law, Section 487 of the Canadian Criminal Code, came into effect on July 1, 2000. On July 11, a twenty-one-year-old woman convicted of assaulting another woman with a beer bottle became the first Port Alberni resident to be ordered to submit to DNA sampling. That data would then be entered into the new National DNA Data Bank of violent offenders.

Because assault causing bodily harm is classified as a "primary designated offence," the Crown counsel for this landmark assault case, Steve Stirling, called on the judge to impose the new measure —submitting DNA to the new data bank—along with a ban on the possession of weapons, although he did not seek a jail sentence. The accused woman was defended by Roddy Patten's defence counsel, Charles Beckingham, who raised an objection when Stirling asked Judge Michael Hubbard to have the accused "detained" so she could provide a genetic sample consisting of "one or more bodily substances." In response, Judge Hubbard, noting that the wording of the law stated "may be detained" as opposed to "shall be detained," ordered that detention not exceed two hours.

Following the court session, Beckingham pointed out that the law as enacted did not even provide for a voluntary appearance for sampling at the police station. On the judge's decision to temper the ruling, he observed, "It's not the judge's place to repair faulty legislation."

This case prompted Beckingham to speak at length on the defects inherent in Section 487, in preparation for his defence of Patten. "Now the state has taken a single mother, and she's in there with all the other axe-murderers and rapists," he observed. In contrast, Beckingham noted, police do not bring a suspect into custody for fingerprinting. "How big a state do you want to have?" he asked, noting that the country had just launched the long-gun registration program as well. Beckingham predicted that the campaign to fill up the DNA data bank would inevitably lead to abuses, both in the collection and in the interpretation of data. He bridled at the standard argument that innocent people have nothing to fear.

"That's what the police always say—'We don't charge innocent people,'" Beckingham said. "That argument says, 'Strip down naked in front of us. If you don't want to, you must have something to hide.' But once the bureaucracy has this information, what's to stop them from using it for anything they like? The fact is, crime rates are dropping in Canada. There is no need to give the police more powers."

THE TRIAL OF Roderick Patten Jr. was set to begin in Victoria Supreme Court in January 2001, almost a full year after his transfer to adult court on a charge of first-degree murder. On Thursday, January 4, a jury was selected, and the trial proper was scheduled to begin with a one-week *voir dire* beginning on Monday, January 8. Then the accused threw the entire process into the wastebasket.

On Monday, when the *voir dire* was scheduled to open, it was announced that on the previous Friday, Patten had hired Victoria lawyer Jim Heller to represent him. He had dismissed Beckingham following Thursday's court appearance. Understandably, Heller immediately applied for an adjournment to give himself time to prepare for what was a complex case by any definition. Justice Allan Thackray adjourned the trial to June 4. Thackray had attempted to find an earlier court date, but the Crown and Heller had previously scheduled commitments over the next five months. The trial was set to last four weeks, with jury selection set for May 28. The judge further publicly admonished the accused for causing a costly delay to the proceedings.

Why Patten parted company with Beckingham is a matter of speculation. Beckingham acknowledged there had been "differences between himself and his client" but expressed his confidence that Patten wasn't using the tactic to delay the trial.

Dan Smith believes that Patten had already planned to change the approach of his defence, and that would necessitate new counsel. At the time of the confession, which Beckingham attended, there was no mention of the future "I-was-too-stoned-to-know-what-I-was-doing" defence. But back in 1997, Tommy George, the Port Alberni man who killed the elderly George Evenson, had raised the issue of excessive drug consumption—successfully—as an extenuating factor in his crime. George was subsequently sentenced to one count of manslaughter.

Dan Smith said there was every chance that Patten had picked up that information while in custody and decided it might work.

Had Patten suggested using the same tactic in his own defence, that would, arguably, have placed his defence counsel in the position of suborning perjury, that is, deliberately placing false testimony before the court. Beckingham had attended a full and explicit confession by his client. I asked Smith if, with this knowledge before him, Beckingham could still have mounted a defence based on reasonable doubt—or if he could have raised the too-stoned-to-be-criminally-responsible defence.

"Oh yes," Smith said. "In my opinion, a lawyer is very much like a judge in that they are able to divorce themselves from evidence that is not admissible. Suppose a judge hears about a confession in a *voir dire*, and rules it inadmissible—he does not now excuse himself and get a new judge. He still hears the trial."

Smith said lawyers are able to make the same mental shift. The presumption of innocence is the foundation of the justice system as we know it. "They may be well aware of the guilt of their client, but they still provide an effective defence," he said. "Hopefully, in the vast majority of cases, the Crown is bringing the guilty party to trial. It is not about whether the accused is guilty. The vast majority of the time, it's about 'How did the police catch him?'"

JURY SELECTION TOOK place on May 28, 2001, in Victoria Supreme Court. In an echo of the Gurmit Dhillon trial, jurors were asked if they could judge the case impartially given the fact that the accused had Indigenous ancestry while the victim was Caucasian. But the main concern, both for the prosecution and the defence, was the extensive pre-trial publicity as the investigation, then the prosecution, had dragged on for nearly five years since the killing across from the ball field in July 1996. In both cases, jurors satisfied both the Crown and the defence that they could render an impartial judgment.

For the Patten trial, Shelley Arnfield served as both file coordinator and exhibit manager and would be a critical player in a bizarre drama that later ensued when the defence was unable to produce a key expert witness. But even at the beginning, her participation was affected by the problems with the case, as when the five-month adjournment caused a major disruption.

"I was there for the whole trial," she said. "As file coordinator, if they needed something, I was the one who knew where, in the file, to find that thing. This investigation filled four 4-drawer filing cabinets. So, when he was supposed to go to trial in January, we crammed everything into two filing cabinets—there was certain stuff we could leave behind, because it wasn't germane to anything—rented a van, and [Constable] Terry Horrocks and I hauled it down to Victoria to the Crown office, where it stayed until Roddy fired his lawyer. Then Terry and I went back to Victoria and carted these filing cabinets back." Arnfield and Horrocks accompanied Dan Smith, joined by Serge Cashulette, who would testify on the discovery of the body and the evidence collected at the crime scene.

Arnfield said there had been some squad-room scepticism about the need for two officers and a rented van to haul a file to Victoria. So when she and Horrocks had to haul the same load back for the trial, she asked a couple of members for some assistance. "When they saw the extent of it, they were dumfounded—they'd had no idea how much was involved. Terry and I were not going down to Victoria with an accordion file under one arm."

VOIR DIRE TOOK place from June 5 through 8, with the trial proper opening before the jury on Monday, June 11. The *Alberni Valley Times* booked me a motel room for two nights so I could catch the opening of the trial.

As a reporter for one of the few remaining afternoon dailies, I had the opportunity to get a jump on the competition and, importantly, file the first bylined story of the day to the Canadian Press. That was going to mean doing some "old school" reporting. Years later, I would be approved to bring a laptop to court in Port Alberni and write stories in real time, but in 2001, electronic recording devices were still prohibited. So like an old-time reporter out of a period movie, I jotted notes down on one legal pad while composing copy on another. Then, during breaks, I'd rush to the bank of payphones down the hall and bark out a more or less comprehensible story to someone on the other end of the line.

The mood was especially tense when I entered the courthouse prior to the trial opening, looking for potential interviews. I spotted Constable Serge Cashulette in the hallway, glaring about in his customary way. I hadn't seen him in months, so I walked up to greet him. Cashulette looked at the brand-new Leatherman multi-tool on my belt. "Dat's a weapon!" he rasped. "Get rid of it!" I ran back out to my car and stashed it.

Dan Smith said he had to meet with the States family before the trial opened. He later explained why: "The most emotional moment for me was when I had to explain to Jessica's parents and extended family members who were also there, exactly how their daughter died. Because much of that was 'holdback' evidence, and so they were never informed, and couldn't be informed, of a lot of the details. They were now going to hear it in trial, so rather than hearing it for the first time in a courtroom, in cold, clinical terms, it might be best to hear it from someone who was involved in the investigation. That fell to me, being the prime investigator." That meeting took place in a witness room at the courthouse in Victoria.

"I gathered everybody around them and explained that what they were about to hear was going to be pretty tough, but here's what happened. I said, 'If it's any comfort, I can tell you that, melding the evidence that Patten gave me with the results from the autopsy, there was a lot that happened to her, but she was almost certainly unconscious while it was happening.' It was very emotional and very tough."

The trial began with Justice Thackray instructing the jury that Patten was to be presumed innocent. "He at no time has to prove his innocence. The onus of displacing innocence is on the Crown," Thackray said.

Opening for the Crown, David Kidd set out the circumstances of the crime and explained that the case would hinge on DNA evidence linking Patten to the crime scene. He told the jury that the evidence would demonstrate that Jessica suffered injuries consistent with a sexual assault and that the DNA profile extracted from semen collected at the crime scene was a direct match to the accused. Kidd also advised that he would, during the course of the trial, present a video recording in which the accused made a full and detailed confession to the killing.

"The Crown is confident you will find, beyond any reasonable shadow of doubt, that Mr. Patten is responsible in law for the first-degree murder of Jessica States," Kidd concluded.

Darrill Prevett, the lead Crown counsel, advised that he expected to call about fifteen witnesses during the course of the trial. He explained that the case would include a significant DNA component, but that with a number of successful DNA prosecutions now on record, prosecutors had by now learned how to present the highly technical evidence. "We don't try to turn juries into scientists," he said. "But I think most jurors by now have a general understanding of the concept."

Patten, hair now cropped short, wore a new suit as he sat behind Plexiglas in the prisoner's dock. States family members and supporters were seated immediately behind the accused. Dianne States, who was scheduled to testify, was not present.

But Heller, the new defence lawyer, threw the whole courtroom for a loop when he announced during opening arguments that his client was indeed guilty of raping and killing Jessica States. At the time of the crime, however, he was too stoned on LSD to form the intent to kill. "Try to put aside the passions which are aroused by the death of Miss States," he urged the jury. Yes, Heller said, his client was a street criminal. "He was in the business of selling LSD. He was a punk, living an undirected life." During a meeting with friends that day, "in a ridiculous macho gesture," Patten took a huge amount of the drug. "He lost the ability to appreciate the quality of his actions," Heller told court. "He awoke to this nightmare too, along with the rest of Port Alberni."

At this point, Thackray interjected to ask whether Heller intended to argue for a lesser charge of second-degree murder. Heller replied that it was a clear case of first-degree murder or manslaughter—nothing in between. "I'm not asking you to let this man go free," he said. "What we have here is not a murder but a manslaughter."

One of those caught by surprise was Dan Smith. "The first I heard of this was at trial. He certainly didn't raise any drug issues during his confession," he said.

WHEN THACKRAY CALLED a break, I raced down the hallway to the pay-phones and called my office collect. I had scrawled out the highlights of the trial thus far, focussing on the sensational tactic introduced by the defence, and dictated them to the production department. Production in turn handed my rough version to the newsroom, where a colleague put together my summation of opening arguments with some boilerplate. Under the headline, "Accused Killer Blaming Bad Acid Trip," the story hit the Canadian Press newswire as expected. By this time, *Times* reporter Karen Beck was managing editor. She had reserved a block of space at the top right corner on the front page.

Also on page one, beneath the Jessica States trial story, was an account of the execution of Timothy McVeigh, the domestic terrorist who was convicted of killing 168 people in the bombing of the Alfred P. Murrah Federal Building in Oklahoma City on April 19, 1995. It was a reminder that Canada had long since abolished capital punishment and that, even if convicted and given the maximum sentence, Patten could conceivably become a free man in his early thirties.

THE FIRST CROWN witness to take the stand was Corporal Harold Vousden, who had served as the identification officer on July 31, 1996, when Jessica went missing. Prevett led him through the time sequence of his arrival at the crime scene and his subsequent departure.

Using crime scene photographs, Vousden described how he first saw the body, covered in bark and forest mulch, well off the main path beneath the bushes in Dry Creek Park. In cross-examination, Heller asked the witness to clarify the terrain. Vousden responded to each question in a flat, measured voice. The death scene was clearly off the main path, in thick brush, he explained.

"All right. I think I finally understand," Heller said. He then asked if the death scene was "exactly as it was found" by search and rescue volunteers.

"I don't know how the body was found by the rescue team—that's how it was found by me," Vousden responded, in the same flat voice. "I understand there was some disturbance of the scene by search and rescue, but I didn't talk to them about how."

After Vousden, Dianne States took the stand. Her voice cracking with emotion, she described the hasty search that took place when Jessica failed to come home from the ballgame on the night of her death. The family contacted police at 11:15 PM. Heller did not cross-examine Dianne States.

Shannon Charlesworth was a volunteer at the ballpark on the night of the crime. David Kidd led her through her observations about that evening. At about 9:15 PM, Charlesworth testified, she saw "Jessie" sitting with "a young male" at a picnic table across the street for the park.

"Did you get a good look at the male at the table with Jessica?" Kidd asked.

"No, he just looked like a regular kid—about fourteen to fifteen years old, kind of hunched over." On further questioning, she added, "He looked partly Native—sort of dark." What colour hair? "Black."

In his cross-examination, Heller attempted to establish that Charlesworth hadn't paid any particular attention to Jessica States that night. But the witness was adamant: she had distinctly seen Jessica on three separate occasions during the evening. "The boy in question—did he do anything to raise your suspicions? Was he looking around furtively?" Heller demanded. No, Charlesworth said, noting that she could not positively identify the boy at the table as Roddy Patten.

Following Charlesworth, the groundskeeper of Recreation Park, Don Barkley, testified that he had found a mountain bike at the picnic table and put it into a storage room. It was not until late the next morning that he realized it belonged to the missing child and that the RCMP helicopter had been searching for it since the beginning of his shift.

Then Alberni Valley Rescue member Stephen Adams described how he had found Jessica's lifeless body when he flipped over a piece of freshly peeled bark as he climbed over a log. On questioning by Kidd, Adams established that the body had been carefully and deliberately concealed under a mound of bark and forest debris. Kidd intended to establish beyond a reasonable doubt that this was not a hasty, spontaneous act by a confused killer.

"If I hadn't moved the bark, I would have walked past it completely,'" Adams testified. With the use of crime scene photographs, Adams identified individual pieces of bark that had been stripped from a nearby tree and placed strategically to cover the girl's battered body.

When a friend of the States family, Corey Porter, took the stand, Kidd led him through his activities on the night Jessica went missing and the following day. "Your honour, I'm having trouble understanding the relevance of this," Heller interjected. Kidd then established that Porter had been called in to identify the body. (By coincidence, Porter was one of the two visitors who had visited Gurmit Dhillon's father at Alberni Foundry on the evening of April 14, 1977, the night Carolyn Lee was abducted.)

With half an hour left on the clock, Kidd advised the court that he had no further witnesses on hand. "Things are going quickly. And that's good," Thackray observed after the jury was dismissed for the day. It was at this point that Heller advised the judge that, because of the speed of the proceedings, he would likely have a scheduling conflict with his expert witness, a toxicologist named Dr. Paul Cooper, who would testify on the debilitating effects of LSD.

"Frankly, I'm in trouble, time-wise," Heller said, explaining that Cooper was scheduled to testify in a pair of trials in Toronto and might not be available until June 25. He asked for a one-week adjournment to follow the completion of the Crown's case. In response, Thackray said he would be "very resistant" to allowing an adjournment, in light of the fact that the trial had already been delayed five months because Patten had hired a new defence counsel.

"If Mr. Cooper has reasons he cannot be here—that he has commitments somewhere else—he'd better give us that in writing, or he'd better be here himself," Thackray concluded.

Now, with the luxury of time and extensive notes, I sat down and composed a lengthy account of the trial thus far, then emailed it to the office. The story appeared in the June 12 edition of the *Times*, under the headline, "Patten Trial Rushes Headlong to Conviction: Manslaughter or First-Degree Murder the Only Question Left." That would serve as the main story, while I would be able to dictate another handwritten account of the next morning's proceedings to run separately.

THE NEXT MORNING, I arrived at the courthouse in righteous anger. On Monday morning, a news photographer had captured an emotionally stricken Dianne States clinging to her husband at the entrance to the courthouse, and it was now on the front page. On Tuesday, at the entrance to the courthouse, I recognized the man who had taken the devastating shot and headed his way. I think I planned to say something like, "That's not the way we do it in Port Alberni."

But the photographer stopped me short. Immediately, I could tell he was equally upset. He mumbled something like, "I know what you're going to say. I feel like hell." We left it at that. In hindsight, it was an excellent news shot that reflected the emotional stakes in the case. But the offending photographer had by now been swept up in that communal feeling that this case was somehow different.

First to take the stand that morning was the original exhibit manager, Serge Cashulette. In a subdued, measured tone, he described the crime scene and recounted the series of numbered exhibits collected at the crime scene, and later, at autopsy. The most significant was the 375-millilitre Meagher's apricot brandy bottle found next to Jessica's lifeless body. Cashulette made no comment, merely holding up the bottle, contained in a plastic evidence bag, for the benefit of the jury.

Shelley Arnfield said that Crown counsels Prevett and Kidd had to adjust their approach as the result of Heller's surprise admission of his client's guilt. "I never testified because he admitted it," she said. "So the trial was, in effect, about [Patten's] mental competency; was it murder or manslaughter? They weren't disputing that he was the [guilty] party." That meant, rather than focussing on guilt, Kidd and Prevett would have to convince the jury that this was not the act of a man incapable of forming the intent to commit murder, because he was "wrecked out of his tree."

"And yet," Arnfield said, "'I'm not so wrecked out of my tree that I pull all this bark off a tree and cover her so she looks like part of the woodland floor.' That's why Serge was testifying—to paint the picture of the deliberateness of the scene where she was found. If you're wrecked out of your tree, you walk away."

Following Cashulette, the forensic pathologist, Dr. Laurel Gray, who performed the autopsy, testified to the extent of Jessica States's injuries and the exact manner of her death. She explained the significance of the bagged exhibit Cashulette had held up. My morning brief focussed on Gray's testimony. I wrote: "Jessica States died as a result of massive injuries to the face and head which were probably inflicted with a small liquor bottle according to a forensic pathologist who testified this morning in the murder trial of Roderick Patten."

According to Gray, Jessica suffered three separate traumas during the assault, any of which would have been fatal in its own right. The first blows from the bottle caused brain swelling, which would have led to death, Gray testified. But the overkill continued. Gray testified that the assailant had stuffed dirt, bark, and forest mulch into the struggling girl's mouth, sufficient to cause death by asphyxiation.

Finally, Patten had jammed a pointed object, likely a sharp stick, into her head, causing a penetrating wound of the brain, equally lethal.

Prevett asked the pathologist if there was any sign of strangulation. Gray said there was no sign of manual strangulation, but there was significant bruising consistent with pressure on the neck. Based on the amount of swelling, Gray concluded that Jessica might have lived from fifteen to thirty minutes following the attack. (Coincidentally, that echoed the pathologist's finding in the death of Carolyn Lee, twenty-four years earlier.)

In his cross-examination, Heller repeatedly attempted to establish that, in a drug-fuelled frenzy, his client was working over a lifeless target, following the initial blows to the head. Gray repeatedly maintained that the unconscious brain-damaged victim would make involuntary movements that could be interpreted as consciousness. "Are you sure you are not just speculating?" Heller demanded.

At this point, Thackray interjected. "I don't know how many times you want to ask the doctor that question, Mr. Heller," he observed, but Heller continued to press. He questioned the blows that Gray had testified were probably caused with the bottle. "Could they not have been inflicted by repeated blows with a fist?" he asked.

"The shape of the injury led me to conclude that it was not made with a fist," Gray replied. On further questioning, Gray said it was likely that the assailant struck the victim between twenty and thirty times.

"So it is likely that the girl was pummelled while she was unconscious and simply lying on the ground?" Heller continued. "The secondary blows ... they weren't inflicted to stop her from getting up?"

"I think that's going a bit far," Thackray interjected. Thus admonished, Heller wrapped up with a few questions about specific bruising and the nature of the plant and soil material found in the body.

The day concluded with a one-hour video deposition from a forensic odontologist, Dr. David Sweet, who had been called in to examine what was believed to be a bite-mark on Jessica's body. In his presentation, Sweet delivered a primer on forensic odontology, followed by a description of the five categories of bite-marks. Based on his examination, Sweet concluded that the "suck-wound" on the victim's chest was of minimal forensic significance. In short, there were no tooth-marks that could identify an assailant.

After the jury was dismissed, Thackray announced that he was forced to comply with the request for an adjournment in the name of allowing a reasonable defence. The jury had not been sequestered.

"Well, we don't want to allow an appeal, do we?" Kidd observed. "You just hope the jury won't forget about the evidence."

Dan Smith was scheduled to testify on the third day of the trial to present the DNA evidence and to introduce the videotaped confession. Kidd said the testimony would be brief and to the point. "It shouldn't go on too long, because [guilt] isn't being contested—he [Heller] isn't contesting the evidence." Of Smith's testimony and the videotaped confession, he added, "Tomorrow is the proof of the pudding."

THE NEXT DAY, the court heard Smith's DNA evidence and saw the video-taped confession, which painted a gruesome picture of the scene. Hiron Poon said he and the Crown prosecution team had prepared extensively for the sort of challenge Russ Chamberlain had initiated three years earlier in the Lee trial. "I did testify at the preliminary hearing and at trial, but I don't think the defence made a big fuss about [DNA] in the end because there was so much forensic evidence," he told the author.

With Patten's guilt a given, it was the confession video that spoke most vividly to his state of mind at the time of the killing. "I had sex with her," the jury heard Patten admit. "She didn't say 'No' or 'Stop.' I never gave her a chance to. I was so scared. It had already started. So scared. I hit her." During the confession, the jury also heard Patten admit to stabbing Jessica in the head with a stick when she wouldn't stop moving. The Crown's hope was that the gruesome admissions would remain vivid in the minds of the jury while they waited for the defence's expert witness to become available.

Near the end of the tape, Smith asked if the accused would like to say anything to Jessica's parents.

"Tell them I'm sorry. I'm so, so sorry. I wish I could go back. I see her picture all over the place," he said. "I've already taken one life, but I can't even take my own. I didn't mean to wreck her life. I didn't mean to wreck anybody's. Sick."

Notably absent was any reference to massive drug consumption, as contended by the defence. When Patten later took the stand in his own defence, he would describe a horrifying, hallucinatory nightmare very much at odds with his portrayal of the scene for Dan Smith and the interview team.

Smith said while his own testimony was "very difficult," the evidence was much clearer than in the Dhillon trial, and the cross-examination much less acrimonious. "I was much more confident this time around that we had done everything correctly. I had some concerns that there were investigation techniques that we ought to have used, but the evidence we had, I thought, was pretty bulletproof." Judge Thackray later commended the team on the quality of the investigation. "I took some comfort from that because I certainly never got those comments during the Dhillon matter."

WITH THAT, THE trial adjourned until June 25, when the defence's expert witness, Dr. Paul Cooper, was expected to be available. Shelley Arnfield said Dr. Cooper's unavailability came as a surprise to both sides, including Heller. Having staked his client's entire defence on drug-induced diminished capacity, his expert witness could now not be depended on. "Nobody knew that until Heller got up in court and said, 'I've got a problem. My drug expert is not available ... I spoke with Dr. Cooper before court this morning ... as he was getting ready to board the plane for Ontario,' Heller told the judge. 'I reconfirmed his schedule with him, told him what Your Lordship said with respect to him staying in touch with me. As soon as he gets to Ontario, if there's any change, if anything folds, if there's a resolution earlier to any of those matters, he promised to me—promised me that if that were to happen—first of all, he's going to contact me, early next week.'"

"Really, what could Judge Thackray do but grant him the time?" Arnfield said. "But then he turned to Darrill [Prevett] and said, 'You need to check into this.' That's when Darrill turns to Shelley and says, 'Find out what Cooper is doing in Ontario.'"

Back in Port Alberni, Arnfield began making phone calls. Allegedly, Cooper was in Hamilton, Ontario, testifying in two criminal cases, one of which was an impaired driving charge. "I phoned the Hamilton Crown [counsel] office and explained my situation, trying to track down these cases that Dr. Paul Cooper is involved in—he's a defence witness. They said, 'We don't know who defence witnesses are. We don't have that information. We can't help you.'"

Arnfield then decided to try Cooper's home number. Perhaps his wife knew where to find him, she thought. "So I phoned his home in Victoria [BC], and this man answered. I said ... 'Dr. Cooper?' 'Yes.' 'Dr. Paul Cooper?' 'Yes.' I identified myself. I said the judge was asking what these court cases were that he was going to be appearing at in Hamilton. And meanwhile, he's supposed to be there [in Ontario]. Heller said he had spoken to him as he was getting on the plane. [Dr. Cooper] said he couldn't tell me about any of these cases because he didn't want to jeopardize any cases he was appearing on."

At this point, Arnfield knew it was a case of contempt of court. "I got off the phone, called Dave [Kidd], and said, "You're not going to believe this. I just spoke to Dr. Cooper. He's in Victoria.'" Kidd immediately asked Arnfield to write an affidavit spelling out the details of her conversation with the errant expert witness.

"Dan [Smith] and I went ... to Cooper's house. We informed him that he was being investigated for contempt of court, read him his rights. We didn't arrest him; we just informed him that he was being investigated." As Arnfield explained, and as was later summarized in the contempt document, "He was having marital problems. He had met this other woman, and he was going to Ontario to see if it would work out. And he jeopardized a murder trial for that." Prevett and Kidd contacted Justice Thackray to advise him of Cooper's deception.

Arnfield then had to take the unusual step of taking a statement from a defence attorney in the middle of an ongoing murder trial. The conversation took place in the hallway outside the courtroom. In part, the informal conference was to determine whether Heller had any idea what his expert witness had perpetrated. Despite the customary wariness between defence lawyers and police officers, Arnfield was convinced that Heller had no idea that Cooper wasn't in Ontario. "He said he didn't [know], and I have no reason to disbelieve him. I think Cooper just lied to him. I don't think it was a ploy on the defence's part ... [Heller] was visibly shaken by this. I don't believe that he knew what Cooper was up to." Arnfield's information forced Heller to scramble for a new expert witness—one who would corroborate the contention put forward by Cooper and, more importantly, who was available to take over on short notice.

Smith said while Heller had thrown the courtroom into shock with his opening statement, in hindsight, it should have been a little easier to predict. "Again, the DNA warrant was pretty bulletproof. By now, we'd gone through the trial-by-fire with Dhillon, so we were well aware that the consent sample could be an issue." At the same time, he reflected nearly sixteen years later, he wished he had been able to follow the plan originally set out by Dale Djos. "I still think that, but for that confession, we would have been in sad shape." Even at that, the confession was obtained thanks to the cold DNA hit. "By this time, we've got experience in writing DNA warrants. In fact, we've got DNA warrants that stood the test in the Supreme Court of BC."

THE LSD DEFENCE

On Monday, June 25, Roddy Patten took to the stand in his own defence to describe a terrifying drug experience, fuelled by his acquisition of a huge quantity of blotter LSD, in which he was (almost) as much a victim as the defenceless girl he raped and murdered. Patten testified that he had acquired the money to purchase the LSD by raiding an outdoor marijuana grow-op. In his report published the next day, Richard Watts, the Victoria *Times Colonist* reporter, captured the guts of Patten's testimony in a one-sentence lede: "One moment Roderick Patten was 'God,' wolfing down LSD, the next he was in a horrifying world where trees and faces kept melting and he was covered in blood."

Patten testified that it wasn't until the following day, after he met up with several associates, that he realized he had killed a little girl. On the day of the crime, he testified, he had been drinking and smoking marijuana and hashish with friends in his apartment. When the blotter acid appeared, he began to portion it out to his friends and took about four or five "hits" himself. At this point, he testified, somebody dared him to take the remainder, between twenty and thirty hits. "I said 'Sure I could, I'm God, I can do it all.' So I just took it," Patten told the jury.

Patten then provided a detailed odyssey of the next few hours as he fled his apartment after the walls began to melt, then blundered around in the street, raving and getting into confrontations with strangers. "Somebody came over to me and put his arm around me. I remember I looked at him and his face, it was like all these wax drops," he said.

Eventually, Patten testified, he found himself sitting at a picnic table across the street from Recreation Park, "watching trees melt around him." A person approached and began speaking to him as he lay on the ground, terrified, after a flock of birds triggered a panic attack. "That's when the person I know now was Jessica came over. I think all she wanted to do was help me up," Patten told the jury. "I think I pulled her pants down [when I was] getting up. I don't know why I did that. I was on my hands and knees. I hit her."

Patten testified he did not remember having sex with the unconscious girl, but he remembered having a stick in his hand. He "may have" stabbed her in the head with it. He recalled being covered in blood. Patten told the jury that he then went to his mother's house and soaked himself, fully dressed, in the bathtub. He later threw the wet clothing into the garbage and disposed of it. (This is likely the genesis of the rumour that Alma Patten knew of the killing and covered it up.)

The next day, Patten said, he met with a friend and they made plans to get more drugs and alcohol. But later, when he met up with the people he'd taken acid with the previous night, they kept talking about a girl who had gone missing at the ballpark. Patten testified that, at this point, he realized the girl at the picnic table hadn't been just another hallucination. In the ensuing days, Patten said he tried twice to commit suicide: once by hanging (he was unable to jump off the chair) and once by drinking snail poison (he only threw up). More frightening, he said, was that anyone who mentioned the crime said they would like to kill the person who did it. When he was later asked by police to provide a DNA sample, Patten said he readily agreed, hoping it would lead to his arrest.

On cross-examination, Prevett attacked Patten's colourful version of the events of July 31, 1996. He reminded the accused that he had given a specific and detailed description of the initial attack with the bottle, followed by the sexual assault and the stabbing with the stick. Could he produce anyone who would back up his story about consuming all that LSD, Prevett asked.

Patten said he could not. "With the crime I'm in jail for now, there is nobody who wants anything to do with me," he said. Prevett continued his cross-examination the following day, demanding to know why the accused had said nothing about LSD in his confession. He pointed out that at the end of the interview, Dan Smith had asked him if he had anything to add. "That would have been an open invitation for you to talk about the LSD you are now saying you took, wouldn't it?" Prevett said, adding that the accused had not offered "one whistle" to police about drugs.

Prevett accused Patten of trying to evade responsibility for his actions by claiming impairment by drugs. At this point, Patten angrily denied Prevett's accusation. "I took responsibility. That's why I'm sitting here today," he snapped back.

PRIOR TO PATTEN'S testimony, there had been no indication that the accused suffered from any intellectual deficiencies. His adult court record for property crimes and assault did not raise any such speculation. And yet, suddenly, Arnfield said, on top of the "too-stoned-to-know-better" defence, Patten was playing the part of an extremely unintelligent person. "He was portraying himself as being quite mentally deficient. I had known Roddy long enough to know that certainly wasn't the case. He was playing a part." She still bridles when she recalls Patten's testimony before the jury. "Roddy ... [tried] to paint himself as [mentally incompetent]. They were talking to him about what month something had happened. He said, 'Ah, I don't know the months of the year ...' I'm sorry, Buddy—the stupid act ain't flying."

Arnfield was asked if she believed Patten had managed to manipulate the defence team into believing he was mentally deficient. "Any time I had dealt with him, prior to this, the one thing I can say about him was that he was totally lacking in empathy in regards to anything—and that is basically the definition of a sociopath. No empathy whatsoever. So did the defence believe he was this mind-numbed individual who doesn't know the months of the year? I don't know. I'm not going to put myself in defence counsel's head and say what they believed or didn't believe." Arnfield said he had managed to avoid exposing himself to law enforcement as a potential murder suspect for three years, and that was no easy feat.

One thing she still finds hard to believe, however, is that, following Dan Smith's testimony, the lead investigator had been sent home. "They—the money people in Port Alberni, I guess—told Dan that he was finished in Victoria," Arnfield said. In hindsight, Smith said that while the Patten prosecution was of consuming interest to him, personally and professionally, it was probably logical to have him get back to his other files. "Essentially, it was more of a matter of cost for hotels and such. I was there as the file coordinator and dealing with the family, as a contact person," he said. "And I was there for the verdict," he added.

ON JUNE 27, Heller's substitute drug expert took to the stand to make the case for diminished capacity as the result of excessive drug consumption. Simon Fraser University professor Dr. Barry Beyerstein, who was recognized as an expert on the effects of drugs and alcohol on the brain, testified that LSD is one of the most unpredictable psychoactive drugs. Beyerstein said he was stunned when he heard that the accused had allegedly consumed up to thirty hits of LSD. The expert testified that the drug could be dangerous for first-time users who aren't ready for the effects. But experienced LSD users can also suffer severe effects if they consume a larger dose than they are accustomed to, he noted. Beyerstein pointed out that Patten's medical record included a history of epilepsy, seizures, and head injury. "You can expect there might be a bigger effect of a drug in a person who has suffered brain damage before," he said.

The Crown's own expert witness, Dr. Paul Janke, took to the stand the following day to refute Beyerstein's testimony. Janke, a forensic psychiatrist with extensive experience treating young drug users, said Patten's testimony indicated that he was fully aware of his environment and "was engaged in activity with a goal in mind." Janke cited Patten's courtroom description of how he had stabbed Jessica with a stick, then covered her body with bark and forest mulch. Factor out the alleged hallucinatory images and this was not a person detached from reality, he explained. The accused saw something that needed to be hidden—a body—and he took detailed steps to conceal it.

In his testimony, Janke refuted Beyerstein's contention that the accused's history of childhood seizures and head injury would exacerbate the effects of a hallucinogenic drug. According to Patten's medical records, his last recorded seizure had taken place in 1994, two years before the crime. Since that time, he had, by his own admission, consumed both alcohol and cocaine, which would typically trigger seizures in epilepsy-prone individuals. But those seizures did not take place, Janke told the court.

Following Janke's testimony, the Crown introduced Wayne Jeffrey, head of the toxicology unit at Vancouver's E Division forensic laboratory. Jeffrey testified about the physical and psychological effects of LSD. On the subject of LSD dosage, Jeffrey explained that a low dose typically produces illusions. A high dose produces intense hallucinations. But a dose of LSD in the quantity described by Roddy Patten on the day of the crime would most likely result in hospitalization, Jeffrey told the jury.

It all came down to final summations on June 29. Prevett hammered home the two salient points surrounding the crime. The *Times Colonist* reporter, Richard Watts, who had covered the entire trial, summarized Prevett's message in a one-sentence lede: "Sexual desire triggered the attack on Jessica States, fear of getting caught then drove Roderick Patten to kill her, court heard Friday." Prevett told the jury that, according to all of the evidence, Patten had two clear goals when he encountered Jessica States that fatal night: "sex and silence."

"He hit her so she would be incapacitated so he could have sex with her," Prevett said. "Mr. Patten, motivated by lust, intentionally killed eleven-year-old Jessica States to silence her in an attempt to escape detection for his horrendous crime." Prevett reminded the jury that the accused said nothing about consuming LSD when he gave his detailed confession to Corporal Dan Smith. After introducing the account of the drug-saturated party when he was dared to consume thirty hits of blotter acid, Patten was unable to produce a single witness to corroborate his story. That included the person he claimed provided the LSD, a one-legged high school wrestler he knew only as "Lefty."

"You would think by now he might have discovered the name of the only one-legged wrestler in Port Alberni," Prevett suggested. (It should be noted that, in the mid-1990s, there was a member of the Alberni District Secondary School wrestling team who had considerable success despite wrestling on just one leg. He was never implicated in the crime.) Then Prevett reminded the jury that Patten's account of how he financed the LSD purchase with an outdoor marijuana grow rip-off was clearly "contrived," because outdoor marijuana is worthless in June; the plant doesn't flower until much later in the summer.

Fighting back, Heller maintained that if Patten should have been able to provide witnesses to the that LSD binge of July 31, then so should the RCMP have been able to locate witnesses. In an echo of the Dhillon trial, Heller suggested that they didn't bother to try once they had the DNA match and the videotaped confession. The RCMP developed tunnel vision, he suggested, focussing solely on the guilt of the accused and not on the possibility of extenuating circumstances.

Heller suggested the LSD-nightmare scenario was the only plausible explanation for how a young man with a criminal record limited to property offences and common assault could commit such a horrific crime. "It just invites the question in lay people: 'What is going on?' 'Is this guy some kind of a monster?'" Heller demanded. "Or is there something else that must have happened to explain this ugly thing?"

Once again, however, Heller reminded the jury, his client had accepted responsibility for the killing and fully accepted that he would be convicted. But that conviction should be for manslaughter, not first-degree murder, he maintained. "No one—not Mr. Patten nor myself—are asking you to let Mr. Patten go," he concluded.

Following closing arguments, Judge Thackray excused the jurors for the Canada Day long weekend. On Tuesday, he would deliver his instruction to the jury prior to deliberation.

THE VERDICT

In the end, the jury took just three hours to find Roddy Patten guilty of first-degree murder. Because he was seventeen at the time of the crime, he would be eligible for parole after ten years, not twenty-five, had he been one year older.

For Shelley Arnfield, one of the most emotional moments took place outside the courtroom, just prior to Tuesday's session. Rob States had prepared a victim impact statement, to be read before the jury at the time of sentencing. But States felt he would be unable to read the statement, so the task fell to David Kidd. Kidd gathered members of the team, including Dan Smith, in the Crown office so he could rehearse his presentation, which would take place after the jury brought in a verdict. "David wanted to get some practice so he could get through it. Oh, lord—he practised reading it to us in the Crown office," Arnfield said. "And when he got up in front of the jury to read it ... I still cannot ... David's reading it, and he got to the line where Jessica said to her father, 'Is there such a thing as monsters?'

Her father said, 'I told her, No, Honey—they're just make believe.' I didn't know how wrong I was.' And David's voice cracked. I had tears streaming down my face."

The *Times Colonist* account of the hearing, which was co-bylined by reporters Richard Watts and Kim Westad, began with Kidd's presentation to the court. Following his conviction, Patten was asked if he wished to address the court, and Patten said he wanted to apologize.

"I would really like to apologize about what has happened. I'm very ashamed," he said, before turning to Rob and Dianne States and starting to say he hoped the healing could begin for the family. That was when it became a little too much for Rob States, according to Arnfield.

"The States ... were absolute grace under pressure. They were the most dignified people throughout that trial. They conducted themselves with absolute dignity. But when Roddy turned around while he was on the stand—'apologizing'—Rob said, 'Don't talk to me, you bastard. You address the court.'"

DRUG EXPERT FOUND IN CONTEMPT

On July 4, 2001, one day after the conviction of Roddy Patten, Justice Thackray found Dr. Paul Cooper guilty of contempt and issued a fine of $2,500. In his ruling, however, Thackray suggested the monetary penalty would prove secondary to the damage he had surely inflicted on his professional reputation.

In his oral findings, Thackray recounted the series of events leading to the trial adjournment, which, he noted, he granted "very reluctantly." On June 18, Heller had informed the judge that he had retained Beyerstein to replace Cooper, and that Beyerstein would be available on Monday, June 25. Thackray then cited Arnfield's affidavit spelling out her unexpected contact with Cooper at his home in Victoria at the time he was allegedly in Ontario. "In a telephone conversation with Mr. Heller, I informed him that I would be giving consideration to what steps, if any, to take with respect to Dr. Cooper, and that Mr. Heller might so inform Dr. Cooper."

On June 25, the day the trial resumed, Thackray advised Prevett to turn the matter over to the Attorney General of BC, who subsequently filed a contempt charge. On July 4, following the Patten verdict, Cooper appeared before Justice Thackray, represented by D.M. McKimm. R.F. Cutler appeared as counsel for the Crown.

The contempt hearing raised another troubling issue that Thackray included in his ruling: "This other problem, as relayed to me by Mr. McKimm on behalf of Dr. Cooper, was that Dr. Cooper had informed Mr. Heller that he could not support the accused's contention that his mind was not capable of forming the intent to murder. I believe that Mr. McKimm said that Dr. Cooper could not testify that there was a nexus between the killing and the use of LSD."

Thackray opted not to pursue the matter of Cooper's second thoughts on the mental impairment defence any further. After Cooper delivered an apology, Cutler rejected McKimm's contention that the apology should "purge" the contempt. Contempt was criminal by definition, Cutler explained, meaning that a simple apology was insufficient under the law. Thackray affirmed Cutler's position: "In my opinion, Dr. Cooper still does not realize the extent of the damage that he did, and he had no concept, at least until he heard the first portion of these reasons today, of the potential that his conduct had to derail the Patten trial," Thackray said.

Besides throwing the trial into confusion, the adjournment led to considerable added costs for the RCMP and the Sheriff's service in the form of extra flights, accommodation, jury fees, etc. It was inexplicable that a highly educated, experienced, and much-sought-after expert witness like Paul Cooper could behave in such a fashion, Thackray told court.

"Dr. Cooper deliberately misled counsel and the Court. This was not a matter of inadvertence. Furthermore, when contacted by Constable Arnfield, he not only continued the deception, but also added to it . . . I expect that Dr. Cooper has put his career into reverse. His credibility, if tested in court with respect to this incident, would make him an unacceptable witness. He is therefore subject to punishment not directly handed out by this Court at this time. Nevertheless,

I am of the opinion that his apology cannot purge his contempt. He deliberately deceived the Court and court officers. He deliberately interfered with the course of justice. He prejudiced the rights of an accused." Finally, Thackray decided, due to Cooper's "clean background," that a fine would be sufficient punishment, beyond the damage inflicted on his credibility and on his future prospects as an expert court witness.

THE MURDER OF Jessica States continues to resonate in Port Alberni more than twenty years later. Jessica's contemporaries are now the parents of a dwindling school-age population. Many will tell you they watch their children a little more closely and don't allow them the same freedom of movement their parents gave them when they were growing up. Because once there was a feisty, fireball of a girl named Jessica ... and then she was gone.

Epilogue

TUESDAY, SEPTEMBER 11, 2001, was going to be a really bad day at the *Alberni Valley Times*, even without a massive terrorist attack in faraway New York City.

On Monday, the *Times* press crew printed their final edition of the paper; their jobs would then disappear. Effective Tuesday, the editorial and production departments would send pages directly to the Nanaimo *Daily News*, where the paper would be printed on their recently upgraded press. To continue as an afternoon daily and hit the press window, the *Times* pages would have to be transmitted in full, electronically, by 10:30 AM. After printing, the Nanaimo crew would then bundle up 7,000-plus copies and truck them to Port Alberni by mid-afternoon.

Unknown to us at the time, but also on September 10, 2001, Harvey Harold Andres, whom as a rookie Dale Djos had arrested in 1976, went to trial for the May 23, 1982, murder of Shirley Ann Johnston. Using the successful Gurmit Singh Dhillon investigation and prosecution as a template, the Andres investigation was the second historic DNA cold case to go to trial in Canada. Andres would subsequently be convicted.

The last edition of the *Times* to be pressed in-house, on September 10, was decidedly mundane: There had been a lethal plankton bloom at a National Aquaculture salmon farm in Bedwell Sound, on the west coast of Vancouver Island. Terry Fox Week was declared in Port

Alberni. A former *Times* reporter was nominated for a writing award. Later that day, after press time, my colleague Mia Vare covered the grand opening of the new West Coast General Hospital, while I interviewed the maintenance supervisor of Alberni Pacific Division on the issue of the contentious softwood lumber tariff charged on Canadian lumber crossing the border into the US.

At 8:00 AM on September 11, feeling like hell already because twenty-odd co-workers had lost their jobs, I walked into the office to find the entire surviving staff in shock. "Good God! Haven't you been listening to the radio?" someone asked, incredulous, when it became apparent I didn't realize what was going on.

Actually, at eight in the morning, Pacific Standard Time on 9/11, nobody was really sure what was going on. There was a TV on in the production manager's office, and we saw the devastation wrought when the two hijacked airliners crashed into the World Trade Centre towers. We had a hard deadline of 10:30 to find something to lead on the front page.

The editor selected the freshest available Canadian Press story: "Officials Plan to Close Borders after US Terrorist Attacks." What was known, by our press time, was that all airline flights had been cancelled, and all trans-Atlantic and trans-Pacific flights destined for the US had been diverted to the nearest Canadian airports—and that was about it. Mia Vare's hospital story and picture, with my softwood lumber story below, were dutifully transmitted to production in Nanaimo under the new system.

The next day, we scrambled to cover how Port Alberni responded to the terrorist attacks while at the same time covering the day-to-day stuff that continued, albeit in an overwhelmingly gloomy sense of unreality. I canvassed local emergency agencies like the fire department, RCMP, and provincial emergency services. As of September 12, there had been no requests for emergency personnel, but later on, a delegation of Port Alberni firefighters would travel to New York to fill in for those members of the New York City Fire Department lost fighting the Twin Tower blazes.

Back in court on Tuesday, September 18, I wrote about a youth who was ordered to provide a DNA sample following his second conviction for break-and-enter. Despite the DNA order, which would permanently place him in the growing National DNA Data Bank, Judge Brian Klaver limited the sentence to one day in jail and one year of probation. While imposing the sentence, however, Klaver warned the teen how advances in DNA technology made future criminal activity unadvisable. "If you break into someone's house, all it takes is for you to touch a doorknob, or for one of the hairs to fall out of your head, and they will catch you," he warned.

The next day, I interviewed a local man, Dave Tremblay, who had watched the World Trade Center towers collapse while stranded at the airport in Newark, New Jersey, directly across the Hudson River. "I was on the runway, coming home. The plane would have left at nine o'clock," Tremblay said. "The pilot got on the radio and told us the flight was postponed, that there had been some sort of accident. Ten minutes later, he said all flights were postponed until further notice." After disembarking, Tremblay made his way to the airport's observation deck, overlooking the Hudson. "We could see the burning towers from across the river. I watched the first tower go down. You couldn't hear it, but you could feel the ground shake. My first thought was, 'I've got to get back to Canada because terrorists don't attack Canada,'" he said.

(As a tragic side note, while he was still in New Jersey, Tremblay's cellphone began filling up with voicemails as the overloaded local cell towers began scrambling area codes and sending messages to unsuspecting people in the area. But Tremblay was unable to access his cell phone until he returned to Vancouver, a five-day odyssey of bus rides and one especially tense border crossing. That's when he realized he had received voicemails from people trapped inside the World Trade Centre. "One was a woman's voice, saying, 'Oh my god, I don't know what to do,' over and over again. The other was a man's voice, in absolute panic." The messages were deleted automatically, so Tremblay had no idea what happened to the terrified people on the other end of the phone.)

AS MY COLLEAGUES and I continued to cover this new world reality while keeping up with the day-to-day stories of everyday small-town life, I did not know that both of Port Alberni's landmark DNA homicide cases were about to pass into history. On September 26, the Honourable Mr. Justice Low announced that he had dismissed the appeal in the case of *R. v. Gurmit Singh Dhillon*. "In my opinion," Low said, "the evidence was capable of persuading a reasonable jury acting judicially that the only rational conclusion was that the appellant was either the killer of Carolyn Lee, or one of her killers.'"

In the appeal document, defence counsel Russ Chamberlain had raised seven grounds of appeal, which included the trial judge's refusal to examine prospective jurors at large on the issue of impartiality arising out of the ethnic origin of the appellant, as well as the validity of the DNA warrant. In a point-by-point assessment, Low refuted each ground for appeal in detail, citing an extended quote from the trial judge's instruction to the jury regarding the probative value of the Crown's DNA evidence. And he completely rejected the "DNA soup" theory that suggested two donors could create a hybrid DNA profile.

Low noted that the jury was required to weigh the witness statement presented by Alice Lazorko, seventeen years after the fact, and the testimony of Sharon McLeod, the former wife of the accused. There was the physical evidence of the tire impressions and the metal particle extracted from the footprint on the victim's jacket. And then there was that "significant scientific match" found between the DNA of the accused and the semen sample extracted from the victim.

Low concluded that the Crown had followed proper procedure in obtaining evidence, including the DNA warrant, and that the trial judge had properly instructed the jury. "In the present case, it was open to the jury to accept the evidence of Sharon McLeod and to conclude that Seiberling heavy-lug tires on all four wheels of the vehicle made the impressions at the crime scene. It was also open to the jury to conclude that these and other features of the evidence, combined with the opinions of the Crown's DNA experts as to the match between the blood of the appellant and the male DNA in the vagina of the victim, made a compelling circumstantial case that the appellant was the killer or one of two killers. My view of the evidence as a whole leads me to the conclusion that a guilty verdict was one that a properly instructed jury, acting judicially, could reasonably have rendered. I would dismiss the appeal."

Gurmit Singh Dhillon is currently confined at the medium-security Mountain Institution, in Agassiz, BC.

Roddy Patten, meanwhile, never filed an appeal of his conviction, and he remains in custody to this day. He has been eligible for unescorted temporary absences since August 11, 2007, and full parole since August 10, 2009. He first waived his right to parole at a hearing in 2007, then in subsequent hearings in 2009, 2011, 2013, 2015, and 2017, electing instead, for unknown reasons, to remain incarcerated.

Patten's incarceration has included stops at Mountain Institution, as well as the maximum-security Kent Institution, also in Agassiz, and the medium-security Bowden Institution in Innisfail, Alberta. In July 2018 he was transferred to the Regional Psychiatric Centre in Saskatoon, Saskatchewan.

A MATTER OF HISTORY

I asked Dan Smith how, on reflection, it felt to be recognized as a DNA pioneer. "It's a mixed bag," he noted. But he shies away from claiming celebrity status. "Obviously, it takes a team to prosecute these things."

Smith also recounted an episode that took place after both the Dhillon and Patten DNA warrants had been drafted and served successfully, and after Jerry Thompson's CBC *Witness* episode, "The Gene Squad," had made him a recognizable figure in the field of forensic DNA. A senior non-commissioned officer in the Vancouver RCMP office contacted him to advise that they had identified "a suspect in one of his investigations" and that he should obtain a DNA warrant—"right now."

"I patiently explained to the officer that we would certainly consider the information, and we would be able to obtain [cast-off] DNA from the suspect, but there were not sufficient grounds for a search warrant." The next day, a second officer told Smith that the inquiring officer had complained to head office that he wasn't taking her information seriously.

"We ultimately did get cast-off DNA from the person that the first officer told me about. And he was eliminated from suspicion." Smith revealed that the Vancouver officer believed she had a credible suspect for the Jessica States investigation. But with the warranted DNA sample in hand, Smith said the antagonistic exchange between the two officers could have become part of a future defence strategy. "Suppose I am on the stand, and [the defence] asks, 'On such-and-such a day, were you contacted by an officer two ranks higher than you, who told you that someone else did this crime?' My response would be 'Yes.'" And this, explained Smith, could have created a "reasonable doubt, notwithstanding all the evidence that pointed to the person that I say did it."

Smith retired from the RCMP in 2008, after thirty-three years, and took a year off. "Then I was asked to come back as a public servant to vet a homicide project." Then, in 2014, he took his current position as court liaison officer in Campbell River, a role he had performed early in his career as a uniformed officer.

AS MANAGER OF the Vancouver RCMP DNA unit, with a staff of twenty-six technicians, Stefano Mazzega would later oversee the most massive DNA investigation in Canadian history, an investigation in which Hiron Poon also participated.

Between 1983 and 2002, Robert William "Willie" Pickton murdered as many as forty-nine women, mostly marginalized sex trade workers, on his Port Coquitlam pig farm. The site search, which involved extensive excavation and soil sifting, as well as the eventual demolition of most of the buildings, cost tens of millions of dollars and yielded a gruesome assembly of clothing, personal possessions, and body parts belonging to the victims. It was believed that Pickton dismembered some of his victims and fed selected parts of them to the pigs, which were then slaughtered and sold. Most of the twenty-seven victim identifications came as a result of DNA analysis.

Poon was involved in one of the more frustrating files in the Pickton investigation. The case revolved around a human partial skull found in Mission in 1995. "At first they thought the skull was from a (male) visitor from India who was murdered," Poon said. "They were pretty sure about it, so they were going to go to India to get a DNA sample from the parents to confirm it ... [But first,] I extracted DNA from the bone. I said, 'This is from a female.'

"To date, we still don't know who the woman was. At the time, Crime Stoppers came to my lab, and we did a Crime Stoppers series on it. Somebody from Ident did a reconstruction of the facial section. But we never found anything until we hit Pickton. That was in 2002. In one of the pig troughs, we found a piece of bone, and we typed it, and it matched to my missing skull." As a result, Pickton was charged with one more count of murder.

POON SAID THE defence handling of DNA evidence has evolved since the trials of Dhillon and then Patten. Part of that is thanks to the improvements in DNA technology, and part of it owes to successive Supreme Court decisions affirming the validity of the science in linking a perpetrator to the crime. He noted that, by 2001, when Patten went to trial and, two months later, when the Dhillon appeal was rejected, the technology had proven itself to the point where a defence counsel would rarely launch a challenge in that direction. "The only thing they could mount was the interpretation. Today, it comes down to, 'Okay. You've got a profile. Now what does it mean?'"

Here, the defence may fashion a wedge to insert in the Crown case, he explained. Interpretation involves yet another layer of expertise from population geneticists that may provide that window of reasonable doubt in the eyes of a jury. But by 2001, the "DNA soup" theory raised in the Dhillon appeal could be rejected categorically, Poon said. "We deal with two or three donors all the time. We have devised an interpretation system that, if there is enough clarity in the profile, we can pull out genetic information from different contributors ... two, sometimes three people ... depending on the type of mixture. "

Ironically, part of the problem with the interpretation of DNA evidence is the very sensitivity of the equipment used to collect and analyze genetic material. Investigators are able to collect DNA from interactions that could be challenged as meaningless in a court of law. "We are now able to collect 'contact DNA.' When you touch an object, I could potentially be able to pick up your profile," Poon explained. "So, what if multiple people pick up the object?"

If an object is of critical forensic value in the prosecution of a crime, and multiple people have been proven to make contact with it, how can the prosecution prove that the accused was the one who committed the crime? "We're dealing with that kind of argument now—that we're presenting a heavily compromised, weak sample— and how can you make an accurate determination [of guilt] from this profile?"

That, however, was not an issue in 1996. "Back at the time of the States trial, we would never consider doing 'touch DNA.' We said if we collected body fluids—saliva or semen or blood—then we will type them. But now we're doing samples you can't see, for example, from the collar of a shirt, to pick up the profile in a groping case. We can use tape on the chest area or on the lapel of the garment to pick up whoever handled it. The sensitivity of the technology has improved quite a bit, and that can drive demands from the investigative perspective."

Poon said the States case was a landmark in that it was the first successful DNA blooding in Canadian history. But it holds another distinction in that the crime scene samples were subjected to four successive levels of DNA technology under his watch. The first analysis of the crime scene samples was performed on RFLP, followed shortly after by analysis on the two successive STR Multiplex systems. In 1998, the RCMP switched over to the AmpFlSTR Profiler Plus system.

Many of the early donors were immediately excluded using the RFLP process. One hundred and seventy-seven were excluded using the STR Multiplex systems. Two hundred and eighteen reference samples were typed using AmpFlSTR Profiler Plus. Having worked on each successive generation of DNA technology, Poon was one of the grizzled veterans of forensic DNA in Canada and, after thirty-five years as a civilian RCMP employee, was often called upon to pass that knowledge to the next generation, until his official retirement at the end of 2017. On the day he spoke to the author, he had just completed a lab tour for a new trainee.

"I explained to him that when I started with RFLP, we typically required 500 nanograms (billionths of a gram) of pure DNA, and it took us six months to do an RFLP case. When we did the Multiplex system—the first-generation PCR system—we needed something like six to ten nanograms of DNA, and it took about two weeks to complete the DNA profile. The Profiler Plus (Nineplex) system went down to half a nanogram of DNA and one week to do the profile. With the current system that we're using, we can do it in as quickly as two days, using 150 picograms." That is 150 trillionths of a gram of DNA. In practical terms, that means the analyst can obtain a DNA profile from a sample as small as twenty-four human cells.

"This is our procedure. I know there are some other labs with even more sensitive technology. But we don't want to push the system too much." The RCMP has decided not to invest in this new super-sensitive technology at this point, based on case law that is evolving in England and Australia, he explained. Their court systems have thrown out cases using that really low-level DNA because, yes, they have the system to detect it, but they don't have an accurate enough system to interpret it.

From a forensic point of view, it is safer to rely on testing and interpretation that has been accepted by the courts, rather than pushing the limit of detection to the point where it becomes meaningless from a legal standpoint. "But I know the science is there now," Poon added. "I believe it will take about five to ten years to mature to the point where you could actually be able to detect multiple people in that mixture."

Amid a recent spate of historic cold cases cracked by forensic DNA, the case of the 1987 murder of a young Vancouver Island couple in Washington State illustrates some of the improvements to the technology and, perhaps, some of the pitfalls. In November that year, while the landmark Colin Pitchfork case was wending its way through the British courts, Jay Cook and Tanya Van Cuylenborg were murdered on a trip to Seattle. The case languished for decades.

Then, on April 11, 2018, police issued a composite sketch of the suspect, based on a new technique known as "snapshot DNA phenotyping." Five weeks later, police announced that they had arrested fifty-five-year-old William Earl Talbott. But the suspect was actually identified after his profile, obtained from crime scene evidence, was entered into GEDmatch, a public genealogy website. Two of Talbott's relatives had filed their DNA profiles on the site. To unravel the family connections, investigators were assisted by Parabon NanoLabs, a DNA technology company, just two short weeks after their service became available. Family members, in turn, gave permission for their DNA data to be incorporated into the case.

CRIMES FOR THE 21ST CENTURY

In Port Alberni, life went on. Over the next few years, the city experienced a pair of precedent-setting crimes. In 2006, two members of the Alberni Valley Bulldogs Junior A hockey club conspired to make a sex video involving an unsuspecting girl. The sex video resulted in the second prosecution in Canada under a new Criminal Code charge, Section 162 (1), referred to as electronic voyeurism. One of the players —the video operator—has since been called up to the National Hockey League by five different teams.

On February 18, 2008, in what became known as the Plenty of Fish killing, a forty-year-old man with a previous criminal record for violence murdered an openly gay, fifty-two-year-old male nurse after arranging a sexual liaison on social media. The accused was the brother of one of former E.J. Dunn Junior High School principal Tom McEvay's four red-flagged students. His 2011 conviction for second-degree murder was later overturned on appeal, but he was reconvicted in 2015.

I left the *Alberni Valley Times* on December 2, 2011, and immediately started freelance reporting, primarily for *Ha-Shilth-Sa*, the Nuu-chah-nulth Tribal Council news service, as well as some public relations writing. By the fall of 2014, I realized it was time to get going on *The Bulldog and the Helix*. That physical landscape in the opening sequence began changing almost immediately, including the demolition of the old Somass Hotel and the fire at the Arrowview Hotel. The *Alberni Valley Times*, which had been purchased by Black Press, publishers of the cross-town rival *Alberni Valley News*, closed down in October 2015.

I feel fortunate in having experienced the last great days of the hard-charging small-town daily newspaper, and to have had the opportunity to report on events, such as the Lee and States cases, that have shaped Canadian history. I built upon the many lessons of those days when I moved to reporting for *Ha-Shilth-Sa*, putting voice to the concerns and aspirations, often equally historic, of the Nuu-chah-nulth people, on whose traditional territory the events of this book took place.

Acknowledgements

N WRITING *THE BULLDOG AND THE HELIX,* I have been able to draw on a wide variety of sources, most of whom I have had previous acquaintance with during my career as a journalist. Those folks, in turn, helped me secure interviews with other significant voices, most notably Donald Blair, Dan Bond, and Hiron Poon.

For the social/economic picture, I am grateful to familiar contacts to whom I reached out, such as former city manager Jim Sawyer, former mayor/coroner Gillian Trumper, and former city councillors Jack McLeman and Lyle Price. Former MacMillan Bloedel executive Neil Dirom provided a detailed account of the "optimizing" process that resulted in the loss of hundreds of milling jobs during the 1980s. I met Georgina Sutherland through my work at *Ha-Shilth-Sa,* and she, along with educators Tom McEvay and Jim Lawson, provided valuable insight into the character of Roddy Patten.

Many thanks to my former *Alberni Valley Times* colleague Denis Houle, who has operated Houle Printing at the old *Times* office since shortly after the press shut down on September 10, 2001. Through Denis, I was able, early on, to retrieve the bulging Carolyn Lee and Jessica States clipping files, and to access the *Times* archives. That those clipping files were compiled so diligently over the years is testimony to how these two heinous crimes impacted the community.

Major thanks to the Alberni Valley Museum and their staff and archive volunteers. I first discovered this civic gem in 1993, while house hunting in Port Alberni. I have drawn extensively from the museum's photo archive to evoke a picture of what the city looked like during the boom years, as well as from the microfilm archives of the *Alberni Valley Times*.

I would especially like to express my thanks to Dale Djos for his unwavering support since the inception of this project. Dale has shared his memories, his files, and his clippings and has made contacts and opened doors along the way.

Thank you, Dale, and everyone who shared knowledge, experience, and insights with me.

Afterword

DALE N. DJOS

RCMP STAFF SERGEANT (RETIRED)

I **WOULD FIRST LIKE** to say a big thank you to Shayne Morrow for taking a collaborative approach in researching and telling these stories that truly needed to be shared with the community of Port Alberni, BC. I first met Shayne shortly after the investigation into the murder of Jessica States turned into a DNA investigation. Working on this book with him has brought back many memories of the numerous serious cases I was involved in during my tenure in the GIS (General Investigation Section)/Major Crime units, twenty-five of the thirty-plus years I spent in the force. Shayne has worked tirelessly, dedicating his time over many years to put this project together. He has been awesome to work with.

I would like to recognize the dedicated work of Corporal Dan Smith, a truly outstanding investigator. Dan played the most prominent role in both of the DNA-related homicide investigations covered in this book, resulting in the successful prosecution of both suspects. During my nine years as the NCO-in-charge of the Port Alberni GIS, I was fortunate to have worked with Dan and many other fine RCMP members. We were indeed a family.

It is also important to recognize the contributions of the many different RCMP units/sections that worked on both of these complex

cases over the years. These members brought some amazing forensic and investigative skills to bear. Special thanks to DNA specialist
Hiron Poon at the Vancouver Forensic Laboratory, who successfully
reverse-engineered critical DNA profiles in both cases, and more significantly, brought home the "cold hit" in Canada's first successful
blooding.

Thanks also to the citizens of Port Alberni, who supported and
believed in our efforts from the onset and stuck by us over the years
as we learned to use this new investigative tool to bring these suspects
to justice. You are part of history.

Index

BORN IN VANCOUVER, SHAYNE MORROW holds a BFA and an MFA in Creative Writing from the University of British Columbia. In 1994, he relocated to Port Alberni with plans of writing a novel, but as fate would have it, he landed a job as a reporter and photographer at the *Alberni Valley Times*. During his fifteen-year stint with the paper, Morrow developed a strong working relationship with Port Alberni RCMP, obtained high security clearance, and gained real-time access to investigators and lab scientists as the Carolyn Lee and Jessica States cases unfolded.

After retiring in late 2011, Morrow worked as a freelance contributor to *Ha-Shilth-Sa* (the Nuu-chah-nulth Tribal Council news service), *Windspeaker* (Aboriginal Multi-Media Society), and for several years wrote public affairs articles for Pacific Coast University for Workplace Health Sciences. He is married, with one daughter, and still lives in Port Alberni.